History–Social Science Content Standards for California Public Schools

Kindergarten Through Grade Twelve

Publishing Information

When the *History–Social Science Content Standards for California Public Schools, Kindergarten Through Grade Twelve* was adopted by the California State Board of Education on October 9, 1998, the members of the State Board were the following: Yvonne W. Larsen, President; Robert L. Trigg, Vice-President; Marian Bergeson; Timothy C. Draper; Kathryn Dronenburg; Marion Joseph; Marion McDowell; Janet G. Nicholas; Gerti B. Thomas; Marina Tse; and Richard Weston.

This publication was edited by Bob Klingensmith, working in cooperation with Greg Geeting, Executive Director, and Gregory F. McGinity, Education Policy Consultant, State Board of Education. It was designed and prepared for printing by the staff of CDE Press, with the cover and interior design created and prepared by Cheryl McDonald. Typesetting was done by Jamie Contreras. It was published by the Department of Education, 721 Capitol Mall, Sacramento, California (mailing address: P.O. Box 944272, Sacramento, CA 94244-2720). It was distributed under the provisions of the Library Distribution Act and *Government Code* Section 11096.

© 2000 by the California Department of Education
All rights reserved

ISBN 0-8011-1488-8

Special Acknowledgment

The State Board of Education extends its appreciation to the members and staff of the Commission for the Establishment of Academic Content and Performance Standards (Academic Standards Commission) for their outstanding work in developing and recommending the history–social science content standards to the State Board of Education under the provisions of *Education Code* Section 60605.

The members and executive staff of the Academic Standards Commission at the time of the approval of the draft history–social science content standards were the following:

Ellen Wright, Chair*; Robert Calfee, Vice-Chair*; Mike Aiello; Joseph Carrabino; Judy Codding*; Daniel Condron; Linda Davis; Bill Evers; Tony Fisher; Jerilyn Harris; Dorothy Jue Lee; Mark Ortiz; Judith Panton*; Raymund Paredes*; Alice Petrossian*; Glenn T. Seaborg; Kate Simpson*; Lawrence Siskind*; Jerry Treadway*; LaTanya Wright*; Delaine Eastin, State Superintendent of Public Instruction; Sonia Hernandez, the Superintendent's Designee; Scott Hill, Executive Director; Sheila Byrd, Deputy Executive Director; Sue Pimentel, Senior Standards Advisor; and Ellen Clark, Consultant.

Note: The asterisk (*) identifies those members who served on the Academic Standards Commission's History–Social Science Committee.

Special commendation is also extended to the leadership of Lawrence Siskind, Chair of the Academic Standards Commission's History–Social Science Committee; State Board of Education member Marion McDowell; Kirk Ankeney, Chair of the Curriculum Development and Supplemental Materials Commission; and Tom Adams, Consultant, Curriculum Frameworks and Instructional Resources Office, whose significant contributions to this document deserve special recognition.

Ordering Information

Copies of this publication are available for $9 each, plus shipping and handling charges. California residents are charged sales tax. Orders may be sent to CDE Press, Sales Office, California Department of Education, P.O. Box 271, Sacramento, CA 95812-0271; FAX (916) 323-0823. See page 63 for a partial list of other educational resources available from the Department. In addition, an illustrated *Educational Resources Catalog* describing publications, videos, and other instructional media available from the Department can be obtained without charge by writing to the address given above or by calling the Sales Office at (916) 445-1260.

Notice

The guidance in *History–Social Science Content Standards for California Public Schools* is not binding on local educational agencies or other entities. Except for the statutes, regulations, and court decisions that are referenced herein, the document is exemplary, and compliance with it is not mandatory. (See *Education Code* Section 33308.5.)

Contents

A Message from the State Board of Education and the State Superintendent
of Public Instruction iv

Introduction v

Kindergarten Through Grade Five

Historical and Social Sciences Analysis Skills 1

Kindergarten: Learning and Working Now and Long Ago 3

Grade One: A Child's Place in Time and Space 5

Grade Two: People Who Make a Difference 7

Grade Three: Continuity and Change 9

Grade Four: California: A Changing State 12

Grade Five: United States History and Geography: Making a New Nation 16

Grades Six Through Eight

Historical and Social Sciences Analysis Skills 21

Grade Six: World History and Geography: Ancient Civilizations 23

Grade Seven: World History and Geography: Medieval and Early Modern Times 27

Grade Eight: United States History and Geography: Growth and Conflict 33

Grades Nine Through Twelve

Historical and Social Sciences Analysis Skills 40

Grade Ten: World History, Culture, and Geography: The Modern World 42

Grade Eleven: United States History and Geography: Continuity and Change in
the Twentieth Century 47

Grade Twelve: Principles of American Democracy and Economics 54

A Message from the State Board of Education and the State Superintendent of Public Instruction

Seventeen years ago the report *A Nation at Risk*, by the National Commission on Excellence in Education (1983), brought squarely to our attention a "rising tide of mediocrity" in our schools. An era of education reform began. The results were somewhat uneven. The reform movement did stimulate important infrastructure improvements: instructional time was increased, high school diplomas came to signify the completion of minimum course requirements, and emphasis was placed on local planning efforts to improve the schools' efficiency and effectiveness. A shortcoming of the movement up to this point has been the lack of focus on rigorous academic standards. The desire to improve student achievement guided the effort, but it lacked a comprehensive, specific vision of what students actually needed to know and be able to do.

Standards are a bold initiative.

With the adoption of content standards, California is going *beyond reform*. We are redefining the state's role in public education. For the first time, we are stating—explicitly—the content that students need to acquire at each grade level from kindergarten to grade twelve. These standards are rigorous. With student mastery of this content, California schools will be on a par with those in the best educational systems in other states and nations. The content is attainable by all students, given sufficient time, except for those few who have severe disabilities. We regard the standards as firm but not unyielding; they will be modified in future years to reflect new research and scholarship.

Standards describe what to teach, not how to teach it.

Standards-based education maintains California's tradition of respect for local control of schools. To help students achieve at high levels, local school officials and teachers—with the full support and cooperation of families, businesses, and community partners—are encouraged to take these standards and design the specific curricular and instructional strategies that best deliver the content to their students.

Standards are an enduring commitment, not a passing fancy.

Every initiative in public education, especially one so bold as establishing high standards, has its skeptics. "Just wait a while," they say, "standards, too, will pass." We intend to prove the skeptics wrong, and we intend to do that by completely aligning state efforts to these standards, including the statewide testing program, curriculum frameworks, instructional materials, professional development, preservice education, and compliance review. We will see a generation of educators who think of standards not as a *new layer* but as the *foundation* itself.

Standards are our commitment to excellence.

Fifteen years from now, we are convinced, the adoption of standards will be viewed as the signal event that began a "rising tide of excellence" in our schools. No more will the critical question *What should my child be learning?* be met with uncertainty of knowledge, purpose, or resolve. These standards answer the question. They are comprehensive and specific. They represent our commitment to excellence.

YVONNE W. LARSEN, *President*
California State Board of Education

DELAINE EASTIN
State Superintendent of Public Instruction

iv

Introduction

The California State Board of Education has worked hard with the Academic Standards Commission to develop history–social science standards that reflect California's commitment to history–social science education. These standards emphasize historical narrative, highlight the roles of significant individuals throughout history, and convey the rights and obligations of citizenship.

In that spirit the standards proceed chronologically and call attention to the story of America as a noble experiment in a constitutional republic. They recognize that America's ongoing struggle to realize the ideals of the Declaration of Independence and the U.S. Constitution is the struggle to maintain our beautifully complex national heritage of *e pluribus unum.* While the standards emphasize Western civilizations as the source of American political institutions, laws, and ideology, they also expect students to analyze the changing political relationships within and among other countries and regions of the world, both throughout history and within the context of contemporary global interdependence.

The standards serve as the basis for statewide assessments, curriculum frameworks, and instructional materials, but methods of instructional delivery remain the responsibility of local educators.

Development of the Standards

The recommended history–social science standards build on the work of exemplary documents from both within and outside California, most notably the *History–Social Science Framework for California Public Schools,* a document strengthened by the consensus that elicited it and nationally recognized for its emphasis on historical events presented within a chronological and geographic context.

The standards reflect guidance and input from countless members of the California teaching community and other citizens who attended the meetings of the State Board and Standards Commission. Their input contributed substantively to the discussions and the drafts, as did the input gathered from the nine directed community input meetings hosted by the Standards Commission throughout the state in January 1998 and from the five field hearings held by the State Board throughout the state in August 1998. At those forums, parents, teachers, administrators, and business and community leaders helped define key issues. Current practice and the state of history–social science instruction in California were also given special consideration during the process. In addition, history–social science experts from around the nation reviewed and submitted formal comments on the first and second drafts. The more than 70 reviewers included eminent historians, geographers, economists, and political scientists. Their input helped immeasurably to strengthen the rigor and quality of the standards.

Highlights of the Standards

With the *History–Social Science Framework for California Public Schools* as a guide to the eras and civilizations to study, these standards require students not only to acquire core knowledge in history and social science, but also to develop the critical thinking skills that historians and social scientists employ to study the past and its relationship to the present. It is possible to spend a lifetime studying history and not learn about every significant historical event; no one can know everything. However, the State Board hopes that during their years of formal schooling, students will learn to distinguish the important from the unimportant, to recognize vital connections between the present and the past, and to appreciate universal historical themes and dilemmas.

Throughout this document, the use of biographies, original documents, diaries, letters, legends, speeches, and other narrative artifacts from our past is encouraged to foster students' understanding of historical events by revealing the ideas, values, fears, and dreams of the people associated with them. Found in archives, museums, historical sites, and libraries across California, these original materials are indispensable resources. The State Board hopes schools will take advantage of these repositories and encourage students' direct contact with history. The standards also emphasize the importance of enriching the study of history through the use of literature, both from and about the period being studied.

Mastery of these standards will ensure that students not only know the facts, but also understand common and complex themes throughout history, making connections among their own lives, the lives of the people who came before them, and the lives of those to come. The statements at the beginning of each grade provide a brief overview of the greater story under study. The overarching statements in each grade and their substatements function as conceptual units: the numbered items under each overarching standard delineate aspects of the bigger concept that students are expected to master. In this way, teachers and assessors can focus on the concept without neglecting the essential components of each.

The standards include many exemplary lists of historical figures that could be studied. These examples are illustrative. They do not suggest that all of the figures mentioned are required for study, nor do they exclude the study of additional figures that may be relevant to the standards.

The standards do not exist in isolation. The *History–Social Science Framework* will be revised to align with the standards, and it will include suggested ways to relate the standards' substance to students, ways to make connections within and across grades, and detailed guidance for day-to-day instruction and lesson plans. Teachers should use these documents together.

Knowledge and skills increase in complexity in a systematic fashion from kindergarten through grade twelve, although no standards exist for grade nine in deference to current California practice in which grade nine is the year students traditionally choose a history–social science elective.

However, in the coming years, the State Board intends to review this current practice.

In kindergarten through grade three, students are introduced to the basic concepts of each discipline: history, geography, civics, and economics. Beginning at grade four, the disciplines are woven together within the standards at each grade.

The critical thinking skills that support the study of history–social science are outlined in the sections for grades five, eight, and ten. To approach subject matter as historians, geographers, economists, and political scientists, students are expected to employ these skills as they master the content.

While the State Board recognizes that it will take both time and changes in policies for schools, teachers, and students to meet these standards, we believe it can and must be done. When students master the content and develop the skills contained in these standards, they will be well equipped for the twenty-first century.

Historical and Social Sciences Analysis Skills

The intellectual skills noted below are to be learned through, and applied to, the content standards for kindergarten through grade five. They are to be assessed *only in conjunction with* the content standards in kindergarten through grade five.

In addition to the standards for kindergarten through grade five, students demonstrate the following intellectual, reasoning, reflection, and research skills:

Chronological and Spatial Thinking

1. Students place key events and people of the historical era they are studying in a chronological sequence and within a spatial context; they interpret time lines.

2. Students correctly apply terms related to time, including *past, present, future, decade, century,* and *generation.*

3. Students explain how the present is connected to the past, identifying both similarities and differences between the two, and how some things change over time and some things stay the same.

4. Students use map and globe skills to determine the absolute locations of places and interpret information available through a map's or globe's legend, scale, and symbolic representations.

5. Students judge the significance of the relative location of a place (e.g., proximity to a harbor, on trade routes) and analyze how relative advantages or disadvantages can change over time.

Research, Evidence, and Point of View

1. Students differentiate between primary and secondary sources.

2. Students pose relevant questions about events they encounter in historical documents, eyewitness accounts, oral histories, letters, diaries, artifacts, photographs, maps, artworks, and architecture.

3. Students distinguish fact from fiction by comparing documentary sources on historical figures and events with fictionalized characters and events.

Historical Interpretation

1. Students summarize the key events of the era they are studying and explain the historical contexts of those events.

2. Students identify the human and physical characteristics of the places they are studying and explain how those features form the unique character of those places.

3. Students identify and interpret the multiple causes and effects of historical events.

4. Students conduct cost-benefit analyses of historical and current events.

Kindergarten

Learning and Working Now and Long Ago

Students in kindergarten are introduced to basic spatial, temporal, and causal relationships, emphasizing the geographic and historical connections between the world today and the world long ago. The stories of ordinary and extraordinary people help describe the range and continuity of human experience and introduce the concepts of courage, self-control, justice, heroism, leadership, deliberation, and individual responsibility. Historical empathy for how people lived and worked long ago reinforces the concept of civic behavior: how we interact respectfully with each other, following rules, and respecting the rights of others.

K.1 Students understand that being a good citizen involves acting in certain ways.

1. Follow rules, such as sharing and taking turns, and know the consequences of breaking them.

2. Learn examples of honesty, courage, determination, individual responsibility, and patriotism in American and world history from stories and folklore.

3. Know beliefs and related behaviors of characters in stories from times past and understand the consequences of the characters' actions.

K.2 Students recognize national and state symbols and icons such as the national and state flags, the bald eagle, and the Statue of Liberty.

K.3 Students match simple descriptions of work that people do and the names of related jobs at the school, in the local community, and from historical accounts.

K.4 **Students compare and contrast the locations of people, places, and environments and describe their characteristics.**

1. Determine the relative locations of objects using the terms near/far, left/right, and behind/in front.

2. Distinguish between land and water on maps and globes and locate general areas referenced in historical legends and stories.

3. Identify traffic symbols and map symbols (e.g., those for land, water, roads, cities).

4. Construct maps and models of neighborhoods, incorporating such structures as police and fire stations, airports, banks, hospitals, supermarkets, harbors, schools, homes, places of worship, and transportation lines.

5. Demonstrate familiarity with the school's layout, environs, and the jobs people do there.

K.5 **Students put events in temporal order using a calendar, placing days, weeks, and months in proper order.**

K.6 **Students understand that history relates to events, people, and places of other times.**

1. Identify the purposes of, and the people and events honored in, commemorative holidays, including the human struggles that were the basis for the events (e.g., Thanksgiving, Independence Day, Washington's and Lincoln's Birthdays, Martin Luther King Jr. Day, Memorial Day, Labor Day, Columbus Day, Veterans Day).

2. Know the triumphs in American legends and historical accounts through the stories of such people as Pocahontas, George Washington, Booker T. Washington, Daniel Boone, and Benjamin Franklin.

3. Understand how people lived in earlier times and how their lives would be different today (e.g., getting water from a well, growing food, making clothing, having fun, forming organizations, living by rules and laws).

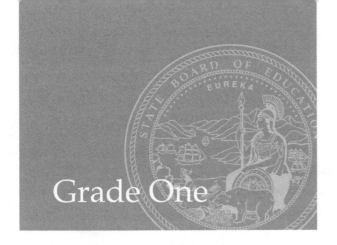

Grade One

A Child's Place in Time and Space

Students in grade one continue a more detailed treatment of the broad concepts of rights and responsibilities in the contemporary world. The classroom serves as a microcosm of society in which decisions are made with respect for individual responsibility, for other people, and for the rules by which we all must live: fair play, good sportsmanship, and respect for the rights and opinions of others. Students examine the geographic and economic aspects of life in their own neighborhoods and compare them to those of people long ago. Students explore the varied backgrounds of American citizens and learn about the symbols, icons, and songs that reflect our common heritage.

1.1   Students describe the rights and individual responsibilities of citizenship.

1. Understand the rule-making process in a direct democracy (everyone votes on the rules) and in a representative democracy (an elected group of people make the rules), giving examples of both systems in their classroom, school, and community.

2. Understand the elements of fair play and good sportsmanship, respect for the rights and opinions of others, and respect for rules by which we live, including the meaning of the "Golden Rule."

1.2   Students compare and contrast the absolute and relative locations of places and people and describe the physical and/or human characteristics of places.

1. Locate on maps and globes their local community, California, the United States, the seven continents, and the four oceans.

2. Compare the information that can be derived from a three-dimensional model to the information that can be derived from a picture of the same location.

3. Construct a simple map, using cardinal directions and map symbols.

4. Describe how location, weather, and physical environment affect the way people live, including the effects on their food, clothing, shelter, transportation, and recreation.

1.3 **Students know and understand the symbols, icons, and traditions of the United States that provide continuity and a sense of community across time.**

1. Recite the Pledge of Allegiance and sing songs that express American ideals (e.g., "My Country 'Tis of Thee").

2. Understand the significance of our national holidays and the heroism and achievements of the people associated with them.

3. Identify American symbols, landmarks, and essential documents, such as the flag, bald eagle, Statue of Liberty, U.S. Constitution, and Declaration of Independence, and know the people and events associated with them.

1.4 **Students compare and contrast everyday life in different times and places around the world and recognize that some aspects of people, places, and things change over time while others stay the same.**

1. Examine the structure of schools and communities in the past.

2. Study transportation methods of earlier days.

3. Recognize similarities and differences of earlier generations in such areas as work (inside and outside the home), dress, manners, stories, games, and festivals, drawing from biographies, oral histories, and folklore.

1.5 **Students describe the human characteristics of familiar places and the varied backgrounds of American citizens and residents in those places.**

1. Recognize the ways in which they are all part of the same community, sharing principles, goals, and traditions despite their varied ancestry; the forms of diversity in their school and community; and the benefits and challenges of a diverse population.

2. Understand the ways in which American Indians and immigrants have helped define Californian and American culture.

3. Compare the beliefs, customs, ceremonies, traditions, and social practices of the varied cultures, drawing from folklore.

1. 6 **Students understand basic economic concepts and the role of individual choice in a free-market economy.**

1. Understand the concept of exchange and the use of money to purchase goods and services.

2. Identify the specialized work that people do to manufacture, transport, and market goods and services and the contributions of those who work in the home.

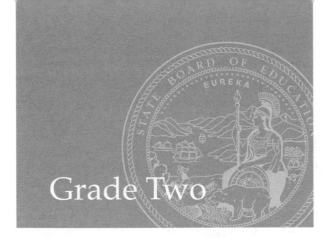

Grade Two

People Who Make a Difference

Students in grade two explore the lives of actual people who make a difference in their everyday lives and learn the stories of extraordinary people from history whose achievements have touched them, directly or indirectly. The study of contemporary people who supply goods and services aids in understanding the complex interdependence in our free-market system.

2.1 Students differentiate between things that happened long ago and things that happened yesterday.

1. Trace the history of a family through the use of primary and secondary sources, including artifacts, photographs, interviews, and documents.

2. Compare and contrast their daily lives with those of their parents, grandparents, and/or guardians.

3. Place important events in their lives in the order in which they occurred (e.g., on a time line or storyboard).

2.2 Students demonstrate map skills by describing the absolute and relative locations of people, places, and environments.

1. Locate on a simple letter-number grid system the specific locations and geographic features in their neighborhood or community (e.g., map of the classroom, the school).

2. Label from memory a simple map of the North American continent, including the countries, oceans, Great Lakes, major rivers, and mountain ranges. Identify the essential map elements: title, legend, directional indicator, scale, and date.

3. Locate on a map where their ancestors live(d), telling when the family moved to the local community and how and why they made the trip.

4. Compare and contrast basic land use in urban, suburban, and rural environments in California.

2.3   Students explain governmental institutions and practices in the United States and other countries.

1. Explain how the United States and other countries make laws, carry out laws, determine whether laws have been violated, and punish wrongdoers.

2. Describe the ways in which groups and nations interact with one another to try to resolve problems in such areas as trade, cultural contacts, treaties, diplomacy, and military force.

2.4   Students understand basic economic concepts and their individual roles in the economy and demonstrate basic economic reasoning skills.

1. Describe food production and consumption long ago and today, including the roles of farmers, processors, distributors, weather, and land and water resources.

2. Understand the role and interdependence of buyers (consumers) and sellers (producers) of goods and services.

3. Understand how limits on resources affect production and consumption (what to produce and what to consume).

2.5   Students understand the importance of individual action and character and explain how heroes from long ago and the recent past have made a difference in others' lives (e.g., from biographies of Abraham Lincoln, Louis Pasteur, Sitting Bull, George Washington Carver, Marie Curie, Albert Einstein, Golda Meir, Jackie Robinson, Sally Ride).

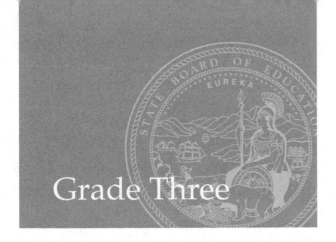

Grade Three

Continuity and Change

Students in grade three learn more about our connections to the past and the ways in which particularly local, but also regional and national, government and traditions have developed and left their marks on current society, providing common memories. Emphasis is on the physical and cultural landscape of California, including the study of American Indians, the subsequent arrival of immigrants, and the impact they have had in forming the character of our contemporary society.

3.1 Students describe the physical and human geography and use maps, tables, graphs, photographs, and charts to organize information about people, places, and environments in a spatial context.

1. Identify geographical features in their local region (e.g., deserts, mountains, valleys, hills, coastal areas, oceans, lakes).

2. Trace the ways in which people have used the resources of the local region and modified the physical environment (e.g., a dam constructed upstream changed a river or coastline).

3.2 Students describe the American Indian nations in their local region long ago and in the recent past.

1. Describe national identities, religious beliefs, customs, and various folklore traditions.

2. Discuss the ways in which physical geography, including climate, influenced how the local Indian nations adapted to their natural environment (e.g., how they obtained food, clothing, tools).

3. Describe the economy and systems of government, particularly those with tribal constitutions, and their relationship to federal and state governments.

4. Discuss the interaction of new settlers with the already established Indians of the region.

3.3 Students draw from historical and community resources to organize the sequence of local historical events and describe how each period of settlement left its mark on the land.

1. Research the explorers who visited here, the newcomers who settled here, and the people who continue to come to the region, including their cultural and religious traditions and contributions.

2. Describe the economies established by settlers and their influence on the present-day economy, with emphasis on the importance of private property and entrepreneurship.

3. Trace why their community was established, how individuals and families contributed to its founding and development, and how the community has changed over time, drawing on maps, photographs, oral histories, letters, newspapers, and other primary sources.

3.4 Students understand the role of rules and laws in our daily lives and the basic structure of the U.S. government.

1. Determine the reasons for rules, laws, and the U.S. Constitution; the role of citizenship in the promotion of rules and laws; and the consequences for people who violate rules and laws.

2. Discuss the importance of public virtue and the role of citizens, including how to participate in a classroom, in the community, and in civic life.

3. Know the histories of important local and national landmarks, symbols, and essential documents that create a sense of community among citizens and exemplify cherished ideals (e.g., the U.S. flag, the bald eagle, the Statue of Liberty, the U.S. Constitution, the Declaration of Independence, the U.S. Capitol).

4. Understand the three branches of government, with an emphasis on local government.

5. Describe the ways in which California, the other states, and sovereign American Indian tribes contribute to the making of our nation and participate in the federal system of government.

6. Describe the lives of American heroes who took risks to secure our freedoms (e.g., Anne Hutchinson, Benjamin Franklin, Thomas Jefferson, Abraham Lincoln, Frederick Douglass, Harriet Tubman, Martin Luther King, Jr.).

3.5   Students demonstrate basic economic reasoning skills and an understanding of the economy of the local region.

1. Describe the ways in which local producers have used and are using natural resources, human resources, and capital resources to produce goods and services in the past and the present.

2. Understand that some goods are made locally, some elsewhere in the United States, and some abroad.

3. Understand that individual economic choices involve trade-offs and the evaluation of benefits and costs.

4. Discuss the relationship of students' "work" in school and their personal human capital.

California: A Changing State

Students learn the story of their home state, unique in American history in terms of its vast and varied geography, its many waves of immigration beginning with pre-Columbian societies, its continuous diversity, economic energy, and rapid growth. In addition to the specific treatment of milestones in California history, students examine the state in the context of the rest of the nation, with an emphasis on the U.S. Constitution and the relationship between state and federal government.

4.1 **Students demonstrate an understanding of the physical and human geographic features that define places and regions in California.**

1. Explain and use the coordinate grid system of latitude and longitude to determine the absolute locations of places in California and on Earth.

2. Distinguish between the North and South Poles; the equator and the prime meridian; the tropics; and the hemispheres, using coordinates to plot locations.

3. Identify the state capital and describe the various regions of California, including how their characteristics and physical environments (e.g., water, landforms, vegetation, climate) affect human activity.

4. Identify the locations of the Pacific Ocean, rivers, valleys, and mountain passes and explain their effects on the growth of towns.

5. Use maps, charts, and pictures to describe how communities in California vary in land use, vegetation, wildlife, climate, population density, architecture, services, and transportation.

4.2 **Students describe the social, political, cultural, and economic life and interactions among people of California from the pre-Columbian societies to the Spanish mission and Mexican rancho periods.**

1. Discuss the major nations of California Indians, including their geographic distribution, economic activities, legends, and religious beliefs; and describe how they depended on, adapted to, and modified the physical environment by cultivation of land and use of sea resources.

2. Identify the early land and sea routes to, and European settlements in, California with a focus on the exploration of the North Pacific (e.g., by Captain James Cook, Vitus Bering, Juan Cabrillo), noting especially the importance of mountains, deserts, ocean currents, and wind patterns.

3. Describe the Spanish exploration and colonization of California, including the relationships among soldiers, missionaries, and Indians (e.g., Juan Crespi, Junipero Serra, Gaspar de Portola).

4. Describe the mapping of, geographic basis of, and economic factors in the placement and function of the Spanish missions; and understand how the mission system expanded the influence of Spain and Catholicism throughout New Spain and Latin America.

5. Describe the daily lives of the people, native and nonnative, who occupied the presidios, missions, ranchos, and pueblos.

6. Discuss the role of the Franciscans in changing the economy of California from a hunter-gatherer economy to an agricultural economy.

7. Describe the effects of the Mexican War for Independence on Alta California, including its effects on the territorial boundaries of North America.

8. Discuss the period of Mexican rule in California and its attributes, including land grants, secularization of the missions, and the rise of the rancho economy.

4.3 **Students explain the economic, social, and political life in California from the establishment of the Bear Flag Republic through the Mexican-American War, the Gold Rush, and the granting of statehood.**

1. Identify the locations of Mexican settlements in California and those of other settlements, including Fort Ross and Sutter's Fort.

2. Compare how and why people traveled to California and the routes they traveled (e.g., James Beckwourth, John Bidwell, John C. Fremont, Pio Pico).

3. Analyze the effects of the Gold Rush on settlements, daily life, politics, and the physical environment (e.g., using biographies of John Sutter, Mariano Guadalupe Vallejo, Louise Clapp).

4. Study the lives of women who helped build early California (e.g., Biddy Mason).

5. Discuss how California became a state and how its new government differed from those during the Spanish and Mexican periods.

4.4 Students explain how California became an agricultural and industrial power, tracing the transformation of the California economy and its political and cultural development since the 1850s.

1. Understand the story and lasting influence of the Pony Express, Overland Mail Service, Western Union, and the building of the transcontinental railroad, including the contributions of Chinese workers to its construction.

2. Explain how the Gold Rush transformed the economy of California, including the types of products produced and consumed, changes in towns (e.g., Sacramento, San Francisco), and economic conflicts between diverse groups of people.

3. Discuss immigration and migration to California between 1850 and 1900, including the diverse composition of those who came; the countries of origin and their relative locations; and conflicts and accords among the diverse groups (e.g., the 1882 Chinese Exclusion Act).

4. Describe rapid American immigration, internal migration, settlement, and the growth of towns and cities (e.g., Los Angeles).

5. Discuss the effects of the Great Depression, the Dust Bowl, and World War II on California.

6. Describe the development and locations of new industries since the turn of the century, such as the aerospace industry, electronics industry, large-scale commercial agriculture and irrigation projects, the oil and automobile industries, communications and defense industries, and important trade links with the Pacific Basin.

7. Trace the evolution of California's water system into a network of dams, aqueducts, and reservoirs.

8. Describe the history and development of California's public education system, including universities and community colleges.

9. Analyze the impact of twentieth-century Californians on the nation's artistic and cultural development, including the rise of the entertainment industry (e.g., Louis B. Meyer, Walt Disney, John Steinbeck, Ansel Adams, Dorothea Lange, John Wayne).

4.5 Students understand the structures, functions, and powers of the local, state, and federal governments as described in the U.S. Constitution.

1. Discuss what the U.S. Constitution is and why it is important (i.e., a written document that defines the structure and purpose of the U.S. government and describes the shared powers of federal, state, and local governments).

2. Understand the purpose of the California Constitution, its key principles, and its relationship to the U.S. Constitution.

3. Describe the similarities (e.g., written documents, rule of law, consent of the governed, three separate branches) and differences (e.g., scope of jurisdiction, limits on government powers, use of the military) among federal, state, and local governments.

4. Explain the structures and functions of state governments, including the roles and responsibilities of their elected officials.

5. Describe the components of California's governance structure (e.g., cities and towns, Indian rancherias and reservations, counties, school districts).

United States History and Geography: Making a New Nation

Students in grade five study the development of the nation up to 1850, with an emphasis on the people who were already here, when and from where others arrived, and why they came. Students learn about the colonial government founded on Judeo-Christian principles, the ideals of the Enlightenment, and the English traditions of self-government. They recognize that ours is a nation that has a constitution that derives its power from the people, that has gone through a revolution, that once sanctioned slavery, that experienced conflict over land with the original inhabitants, and that experienced a westward movement that took its people across the continent. Studying the cause, course, and consequences of the early explorations through the War for Independence and western expansion is central to students' fundamental understanding of how the principles of the American republic form the basis of a pluralistic society in which individual rights are secured.

5.1 Students describe the major pre-Columbian settlements, including the cliff dwellers and pueblo people of the desert Southwest, the American Indians of the Pacific Northwest, the nomadic nations of the Great Plains, and the woodland peoples east of the Mississippi River.

1. Describe how geography and climate influenced the way various nations lived and adjusted to the natural environment, including locations of villages, the distinct structures that they built, and how they obtained food, clothing, tools, and utensils.

2. Describe their varied customs and folklore traditions.

3. Explain their varied economies and systems of government.

5.2   Students trace the routes of early explorers and describe the early explorations of the Americas.

1. Describe the entrepreneurial characteristics of early explorers (e.g., Christopher Columbus, Francisco Vásquez de Coronado) and the technological developments that made sea exploration by latitude and longitude possible (e.g., compass, sextant, astrolabe, seaworthy ships, chronometers, gunpowder).

2. Explain the aims, obstacles, and accomplishments of the explorers, sponsors, and leaders of key European expeditions and the reasons Europeans chose to explore and colonize the world (e.g., the Spanish Reconquista, the Protestant Reformation, the Counter Reformation).

3. Trace the routes of the major land explorers of the United States, the distances traveled by explorers, and the Atlantic trade routes that linked Africa, the West Indies, the British colonies, and Europe.

4. Locate on maps of North and South America land claimed by Spain, France, England, Portugal, the Netherlands, Sweden, and Russia.

5.3   Students describe the cooperation and conflict that existed among the American Indians and between the Indian nations and the new settlers.

1. Describe the competition among the English, French, Spanish, Dutch, and Indian nations for control of North America.

2. Describe the cooperation that existed between the colonists and Indians during the 1600s and 1700s (e.g., in agriculture, the fur trade, military alliances, treaties, cultural interchanges).

3. Examine the conflicts before the Revolutionary War (e.g., the Pequot and King Philip's Wars in New England, the Powhatan Wars in Virginia, the French and Indian War).

4. Discuss the role of broken treaties and massacres and the factors that led to the Indians' defeat, including the resistance of Indian nations to encroachments and assimilation (e.g., the story of the Trail of Tears).

5. Describe the internecine Indian conflicts, including the competing claims for control of lands (e.g., actions of the Iroquois, Huron, Lakota [Sioux]).

6. Explain the influence and achievements of significant leaders of the time (e.g., John Marshall, Andrew Jackson, Chief Tecumseh, Chief Logan, Chief John Ross, Sequoyah).

5.4   Students understand the political, religious, social, and economic institutions that evolved in the colonial era.

1. Understand the influence of location and physical setting on the founding of the original 13 colonies, and identify on a map the locations of the colonies and of the American Indian nations already inhabiting these areas.

2. Identify the major individuals and groups responsible for the founding of the various colonies and the reasons for their founding (e.g., John Smith, Virginia; Roger Williams, Rhode Island; William Penn, Pennsylvania; Lord Baltimore, Maryland; William Bradford, Plymouth; John Winthrop, Massachusetts).

3. Describe the religious aspects of the earliest colonies (e.g., Puritanism in Massachu- setts, Anglicanism in Virginia, Catholicism in Maryland, Quakerism in Pennsylvania).

4. Identify the significance and leaders of the First Great Awakening, which marked a shift in religious ideas, practices, and allegiances in the colonial period, the growth of religious toleration, and free exercise of religion.

5. Understand how the British colonial period created the basis for the development of political self-government and a free-market economic system and the differences between the British, Spanish, and French colonial systems.

6. Describe the introduction of slavery into America, the responses of slave families to their condition, the ongoing struggle between proponents and opponents of slavery, and the gradual institutionalization of slavery in the South.

7. Explain the early democratic ideas and practices that emerged during the colonial period, including the significance of representative assemblies and town meetings.

5.5   Students explain the causes of the American Revolution.

1. Understand how political, religious, and economic ideas and interests brought about the Revolution (e.g., resistance to imperial policy, the Stamp Act, the Townshend Acts, taxes on tea, Coercive Acts).

2. Know the significance of the first and second Continental Congresses and of the Committees of Correspondence.

3. Understand the people and events associated with the drafting and signing of the Declaration of Independence and the document's significance, including the key political concepts it embodies, the origins of those concepts, and its role in severing ties with Great Britain.

4. Describe the views, lives, and impact of key individuals during this period (e.g., King George III, Patrick Henry, Thomas Jefferson, George Washington, Benjamin Franklin, John Adams).

5.6 Students understand the course and consequences of the American Revolution.

1. Identify and map the major military battles, campaigns, and turning points of the Revolutionary War, the roles of the American and British leaders, and the Indian leaders' alliances on both sides.

2. Describe the contributions of France and other nations and of individuals to the outcome of the Revolution (e.g., Benjamin Franklin's negotiations with the French, the French navy, the Treaty of Paris, The Netherlands, Russia, the Marquis Marie Joseph de Lafayette, Tadeusz Kościuszko, Baron Friedrich Wilhelm von Steuben).

3. Identify the different roles women played during the Revolution (e.g., Abigail Adams, Martha Washington, Molly Pitcher, Phillis Wheatley, Mercy Otis Warren).

4. Understand the personal impact and economic hardship of the war on families, problems of financing the war, wartime inflation, and laws against hoarding goods and materials and profiteering.

5. Explain how state constitutions that were established after 1776 embodied the ideals of the American Revolution and helped serve as models for the U.S. Constitution.

6. Demonstrate knowledge of the significance of land policies developed under the Continental Congress (e.g., sale of western lands, the Northwest Ordinance of 1787) and those policies' impact on American Indians' land.

7. Understand how the ideals set forth in the Declaration of Independence changed the way people viewed slavery.

5.7 Students describe the people and events associated with the development of the U.S. Constitution and analyze the Constitution's significance as the foundation of the American republic.

1. List the shortcomings of the Articles of Confederation as set forth by their critics.

2. Explain the significance of the new Constitution of 1787, including the struggles over its ratification and the reasons for the addition of the Bill of Rights.

3. Understand the fundamental principles of American constitutional democracy, including how the government derives its power from the people and the primacy of individual liberty.

4. Understand how the Constitution is designed to secure our liberty by both empowering and limiting central government and compare the powers granted to citizens, Congress, the president, and the Supreme Court with those reserved to the states.

5. Discuss the meaning of the American creed that calls on citizens to safeguard the liberty of individual Americans within a unified nation, to respect the rule of law, and to preserve the Constitution.

6. Know the songs that express American ideals (e.g., "America the Beautiful," "The Star Spangled Banner").

5.8 **Students trace the colonization, immigration, and settlement patterns of the American people from 1789 to the mid-1800s, with emphasis on the role of economic incentives, effects of the physical and political geography, and transportation systems.**

1. Discuss the waves of immigrants from Europe between 1789 and 1850 and their modes of transportation into the Ohio and Mississippi Valleys and through the Cumberland Gap (e.g., overland wagons, canals, flatboats, steamboats).

2. Name the states and territories that existed in 1850 and identify their locations and major geographical features (e.g., mountain ranges, principal rivers, dominant plant regions).

3. Demonstrate knowledge of the explorations of the trans-Mississippi West following the Louisiana Purchase (e.g., Meriwether Lewis and William Clark, Zebulon Pike, John Fremont).

4. Discuss the experiences of settlers on the overland trails to the West (e.g., location of the routes; purpose of the journeys; the influence of the terrain, rivers, vegetation, and climate; life in the territories at the end of these trails).

5. Describe the continued migration of Mexican settlers into Mexican territories of the West and Southwest.

6. Relate how and when California, Texas, Oregon, and other western lands became part of the United States, including the significance of the Texas War for Independence and the Mexican-American War.

5.9 **Students know the location of the current 50 states and the names of their capitals.**

Grades Six Through Eight

Historical and Social Sciences Analysis Skills

The intellectual skills noted below are to be learned through, and applied to, the content standards for grades six through eight. They are to be assessed *only in conjunction with* the content standards in grades six through eight.

In addition to the standards for grades six through eight, students demonstrate the following intellectual reasoning, reflection, and research skills:

Chronological and Spatial Thinking

1. Students explain how major events are related to one another in time.
2. Students construct various time lines of key events, people, and periods of the historical era they are studying.
3. Students use a variety of maps and documents to identify physical and cultural features of neighborhoods, cities, states, and countries and to explain the historical migration of people, expansion and disintegration of empires, and the growth of economic systems.

Research, Evidence, and Point of View

1. Students frame questions that can be answered by historical study and research.
2. Students distinguish fact from opinion in historical narratives and stories.
3. Students distinguish relevant from irrelevant information, essential from incidental information, and verifiable from unverifiable information in historical narratives and stories.
4. Students assess the credibility of primary and secondary sources and draw sound conclusions from them.
5. Students detect the different historical points of view on historical events and determine the context in which the historical statements were made (the questions asked, sources used, author's perspectives).

Historical Interpretation

1. Students explain the central issues and problems from the past, placing people and events in a matrix of time and place.

2. Students understand and distinguish cause, effect, sequence, and correlation in historical events, including the long- and short-term causal relations.

3. Students explain the sources of historical continuity and how the combination of ideas and events explains the emergence of new patterns.

4. Students recognize the role of chance, oversight, and error in history.

5. Students recognize that interpretations of history are subject to change as new information is uncovered.

6. Students interpret basic indicators of economic performance and conduct cost-benefit analyses of economic and political issues.

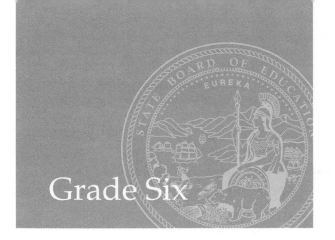

Grade Six

World History and Geography: Ancient Civilizations

Students in grade six expand their understanding of history by studying the people and events that ushered in the dawn of the major Western and non-Western ancient civilizations. Geography is of special significance in the development of the human story. Continued emphasis is placed on the everyday lives, problems, and accomplishments of people, their role in developing social, economic, and political structures, as well as in establishing and spreading ideas that helped transform the world forever. Students develop higher levels of critical thinking by considering why civilizations developed where and when they did, why they became dominant, and why they declined. Students analyze the interactions among the various cultures, emphasizing their enduring contributions and the link, despite time, between the contemporary and ancient worlds.

6.1 **Students describe what is known through archaeological studies of the early physical and cultural development of humankind from the Paleolithic era to the agricultural revolution.**

1. Describe the hunter-gatherer societies, including the development of tools and the use of fire.

2. Identify the locations of human communities that populated the major regions of the world and describe how humans adapted to a variety of environments.

3. Discuss the climatic changes and human modifications of the physical environment that gave rise to the domestication of plants and animals and new sources of clothing and shelter.

6.2 **Students analyze the geographic, political, economic, religious, and social structures of the early civilizations of Mesopotamia, Egypt, and Kush.**

1. Locate and describe the major river systems and discuss the physical settings that supported permanent settlement and early civilizations.

2. Trace the development of agricultural techniques that permitted the production of economic surplus and the emergence of cities as centers of culture and power.

3. Understand the relationship between religion and the social and political order in Mesopotamia and Egypt.

4. Know the significance of Hammurabi's Code.

5. Discuss the main features of Egyptian art and architecture.

6. Describe the role of Egyptian trade in the eastern Mediterranean and Nile valley.

7. Understand the significance of Queen Hatshepsut and Ramses the Great.

8. Identify the location of the Kush civilization and describe its political, commercial, and cultural relations with Egypt.

9. Trace the evolution of language and its written forms.

6.3 **Students analyze the geographic, political, economic, religious, and social structures of the Ancient Hebrews.**

1. Describe the origins and significance of Judaism as the first monotheistic religion based on the concept of one God who sets down moral laws for humanity.

2. Identify the sources of the ethical teachings and central beliefs of Judaism (the Hebrew Bible, the Commentaries): belief in God, observance of law, practice of the concepts of righteousness and justice, and importance of study; and describe how the ideas of the Hebrew traditions are reflected in the moral and ethical traditions of Western civilization.

3. Explain the significance of Abraham, Moses, Naomi, Ruth, David, and Yohanan ben Zaccai in the development of the Jewish religion.

4. Discuss the locations of the settlements and movements of Hebrew peoples, including the Exodus and their movement to and from Egypt, and outline the significance of the Exodus to the Jewish and other people.

5. Discuss how Judaism survived and developed despite the continuing dispersion of much of the Jewish population from Jerusalem and the rest of Israel after the destruction of the second Temple in A.D. 70.

6.4 **Students analyze the geographic, political, economic, religious, and social structures of the early civilizations of Ancient Greece.**

1. Discuss the connections between geography and the development of city-states in the region of the Aegean Sea, including patterns of trade and commerce among Greek city-states and within the wider Mediterranean region.

2. Trace the transition from tyranny and oligarchy to early democratic forms of government and back to dictatorship in ancient Greece, including the significance of the invention of the idea of citizenship (e.g., from *Pericles' Funeral Oration*).

3. State the key differences between Athenian, or direct, democracy and representative democracy.

4. Explain the significance of Greek mythology to the everyday life of people in the region and how Greek literature continues to permeate our literature and language today, drawing from Greek mythology and epics, such as Homer's *Iliad* and *Odyssey*, and from *Aesop's Fables*.

5. Outline the founding, expansion, and political organization of the Persian Empire.

6. Compare and contrast life in Athens and Sparta, with emphasis on their roles in the Persian and Peloponnesian Wars.

7. Trace the rise of Alexander the Great and the spread of Greek culture eastward and into Egypt.

8. Describe the enduring contributions of important Greek figures in the arts and sciences (e.g., Hypatia, Socrates, Plato, Aristotle, Euclid, Thucydides).

6.5 **Students analyze the geographic, political, economic, religious, and social structures of the early civilizations of India.**

1. Locate and describe the major river system and discuss the physical setting that supported the rise of this civilization.

2. Discuss the significance of the Aryan invasions.

3. Explain the major beliefs and practices of Brahmanism in India and how they evolved into early Hinduism.

4. Outline the social structure of the caste system.

5. Know the life and moral teachings of Buddha and how Buddhism spread in India, Ceylon, and Central Asia.

6. Describe the growth of the Maurya empire and the political and moral achievements of the emperor Asoka.

7. Discuss important aesthetic and intellectual traditions (e.g., Sanskrit literature, including the *Bhagavad Gita*; medicine; metallurgy; and mathematics, including Hindu-Arabic numerals and the zero).

6.6 Students analyze the geographic, political, economic, religious, and social structures of the early civilizations of China.

1. Locate and describe the origins of Chinese civilization in the Huang-He Valley during the Shang Dynasty.

2. Explain the geographic features of China that made governance and the spread of ideas and goods difficult and served to isolate the country from the rest of the world.

3. Know about the life of Confucius and the fundamental teachings of Confucianism and Taoism.

4. Identify the political and cultural problems prevalent in the time of Confucius and how he sought to solve them.

5. List the policies and achievements of the emperor Shi Huangdi in unifying northern China under the Qin Dynasty.

6. Detail the political contributions of the Han Dynasty to the development of the imperial bureaucratic state and the expansion of the empire.

7. Cite the significance of the trans-Eurasian "silk roads" in the period of the Han Dynasty and Roman Empire and their locations.

8. Describe the diffusion of Buddhism northward to China during the Han Dynasty.

6.7 Students analyze the geographic, political, economic, religious, and social structures during the development of Rome.

1. Identify the location and describe the rise of the Roman Republic, including the importance of such mythical and historical figures as Aeneas, Romulus and Remus, Cincinnatus, Julius Caesar, and Cicero.

2. Describe the government of the Roman Republic and its significance (e.g., written constitution and tripartite government, checks and balances, civic duty).

3. Identify the location of and the political and geographic reasons for the growth of Roman territories and expansion of the empire, including how the empire fostered economic growth through the use of currency and trade routes.

4. Discuss the influence of Julius Caesar and Augustus in Rome's transition from republic to empire.

5. Trace the migration of Jews around the Mediterranean region and the effects of their conflict with the Romans, including the Romans' restrictions on their right to live in Jerusalem.

6. Note the origins of Christianity in the Jewish Messianic prophecies, the life and teachings of Jesus of Nazareth as described in the New Testament, and the contribution of St. Paul the Apostle to the definition and spread of Christian beliefs (e.g., belief in the Trinity, resurrection, salvation).

7. Describe the circumstances that led to the spread of Christianity in Europe and other Roman territories.

8. Discuss the legacies of Roman art and architecture, technology and science, literature, language, and law.

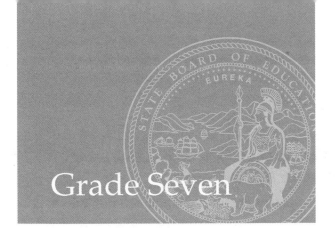

Grade Seven

World History and Geography:
Medieval and Early Modern Times

Students in grade seven study the social, cultural, and technological changes that oc-curred in Europe, Africa, and Asia in the years A.D. 500–1789. After reviewing the an-cient world and the ways in which archaeologists and historians uncover the past, students study the history and geography of great civilizations that were developing concurrently throughout the world during medieval and early modern times. They examine the growing economic interaction among civilizations as well as the exchange of ideas, beliefs, technologies, and commodities. They learn about the resulting growth of Enlightenment philosophy and the new examination of the concepts of reason and authority, the natural rights of human beings and the divine right of kings, experimen-talism in science, and the dogma of belief. Finally, students assess the political forces let loose by the Enlightenment, particularly the rise of democratic ideas, and they learn about the continuing influence of these ideas in the world today.

7.1 Students analyze the causes and effects of the vast expansion and ultimate disintegration of the Roman Empire.

1. Study the early strengths and lasting contributions of Rome (e.g., significance of Roman citizenship; rights under Roman law; Roman art, architecture, engineering, and philosophy; preservation and transmission of Christianity) and its ultimate internal weaknesses (e.g., rise of autonomous military powers within the empire, undermining of citizenship by the growth of corruption and slavery, lack of education, and distribu-tion of news).

2. Discuss the geographic borders of the empire at its height and the factors that threat-ened its territorial cohesion.

3. Describe the establishment by Constantine of the new capital in Constantinople and the development of the Byzantine Empire, with an emphasis on the consequences of the development of two distinct European civilizations, Eastern Orthodox and Roman Catholic, and their two distinct views on church-state relations.

7.2 Students analyze the geographic, political, economic, religious, and social structures of the civilizations of Islam in the Middle Ages.

1. Identify the physical features and describe the climate of the Arabian peninsula, its relationship to surrounding bodies of land and water, and nomadic and sedentary ways of life.

2. Trace the origins of Islam and the life and teachings of Muhammad, including Islamic teachings on the connection with Judaism and Christianity.

3. Explain the significance of the Qur'an and the Sunnah as the primary sources of Islamic beliefs, practice, and law, and their influence in Muslims' daily life.

4. Discuss the expansion of Muslim rule through military conquests and treaties, emphasizing the cultural blending within Muslim civilization and the spread and acceptance of Islam and the Arabic language.

5. Describe the growth of cities and the establishment of trade routes among Asia, Africa, and Europe, the products and inventions that traveled along these routes (e.g., spices, textiles, paper, steel, new crops), and the role of merchants in Arab society.

6. Understand the intellectual exchanges among Muslim scholars of Eurasia and Africa and the contributions Muslim scholars made to later civilizations in the areas of science, geography, mathematics, philosophy, medicine, art, and literature.

7.3 Students analyze the geographic, political, economic, religious, and social structures of the civilizations of China in the Middle Ages.

1. Describe the reunification of China under the Tang Dynasty and reasons for the spread of Buddhism in Tang China, Korea, and Japan.

2. Describe agricultural, technological, and commercial developments during the Tang and Sung periods.

3. Analyze the influences of Confucianism and changes in Confucian thought during the Sung and Mongol periods.

4. Understand the importance of both overland trade and maritime expeditions between China and other civilizations in the Mongol Ascendancy and Ming Dynasty.

5. Trace the historic influence of such discoveries as tea, the manufacture of paper, wood-block printing, the compass, and gunpowder.

6. Describe the development of the imperial state and the scholar-official class.

7.4 Students analyze the geographic, political, economic, religious, and social structures of the sub-Saharan civilizations of Ghana and Mali in Medieval Africa.

1. Study the Niger River and the relationship of vegetation zones of forest, savannah, and desert to trade in gold, salt, food, and slaves; and the growth of the Ghana and Mali empires.

2. Analyze the importance of family, labor specialization, and regional commerce in the development of states and cities in West Africa.

3. Describe the role of the trans-Saharan caravan trade in the changing religious and cultural characteristics of West Africa and the influence of Islamic beliefs, ethics, and law.

4. Trace the growth of the Arabic language in government, trade, and Islamic scholarship in West Africa.

5. Describe the importance of written and oral traditions in the transmission of African history and culture.

7.5   Students analyze the geographic, political, economic, religious, and social structures of the civilizations of Medieval Japan.

1. Describe the significance of Japan's proximity to China and Korea and the intellectual, linguistic, religious, and philosophical influence of those countries on Japan.

2. Discuss the reign of Prince Shotoku of Japan and the characteristics of Japanese society and family life during his reign.

3. Describe the values, social customs, and traditions prescribed by the lord-vassal system consisting of *shogun, daimyo,* and *samurai* and the lasting influence of the warrior code in the twentieth century.

4. Trace the development of distinctive forms of Japanese Buddhism.

5. Study the ninth and tenth centuries' golden age of literature, art, and drama and its lasting effects on culture today, including Murasaki Shikibu's *Tale of Genji.*

6. Analyze the rise of a military society in the late twelfth century and the role of the samurai in that society.

7.6   Students analyze the geographic, political, economic, religious, and social structures of the civilizations of Medieval Europe.

1. Study the geography of the Europe and the Eurasian land mass, including its location, topography, waterways, vegetation, and climate and their relationship to ways of life in Medieval Europe.

2. Describe the spread of Christianity north of the Alps and the roles played by the early church and by monasteries in its diffusion after the fall of the western half of the Roman Empire.

3. Understand the development of feudalism, its role in the medieval European economy, the way in which it was influenced by physical geography (the role of the manor and the growth of towns), and how feudal relationships provided the foundation of political order.

4. Demonstrate an understanding of the conflict and cooperation between the Papacy and European monarchs (e.g., Charlemagne, Gregory VII, Emperor Henry IV).

5. Know the significance of developments in medieval English legal and constitutional practices and their importance in the rise of modern democratic thought and representative institutions (e.g., Magna Carta, parliament, development of habeas corpus, an independent judiciary in England).

6. Discuss the causes and course of the religious Crusades and their effects on the Christian, Muslim, and Jewish populations in Europe, with emphasis on the increasing contact by Europeans with cultures of the Eastern Mediterranean world.

7. Map the spread of the bubonic plague from Central Asia to China, the Middle East, and Europe and describe its impact on global population.

8. Understand the importance of the Catholic church as a political, intellectual, and aesthetic institution (e.g., founding of universities, political and spiritual roles of the clergy, creation of monastic and mendicant religious orders, preservation of the Latin language and religious texts, St. Thomas Aquinas's synthesis of classical philosophy with Christian theology, and the concept of "natural law").

9. Know the history of the decline of Muslim rule in the Iberian Peninsula that culminated in the Reconquista and the rise of Spanish and Portuguese kingdoms.

7.7   Students compare and contrast the geographic, political, economic, religious, and social structures of the Meso-American and Andean civilizations.

1. Study the locations, landforms, and climates of Mexico, Central America, and South America and their effects on Mayan, Aztec, and Incan economies, trade, and development of urban societies.

2. Study the roles of people in each society, including class structures, family life, warfare, religious beliefs and practices, and slavery.

3. Explain how and where each empire arose and how the Aztec and Incan empires were defeated by the Spanish.

4. Describe the artistic and oral traditions and architecture in the three civilizations.

5. Describe the Meso-American achievements in astronomy and mathematics, including the development of the calendar and the Meso-American knowledge of seasonal changes to the civilizations' agricultural systems.

7.8   Students analyze the origins, accomplishments, and geographic diffusion of the Renaissance.

1. Describe the way in which the revival of classical learning and the arts fostered a new interest in humanism (i.e., a balance between intellect and religious faith).

2. Explain the importance of Florence in the early stages of the Renaissance and the growth of independent trading cities (e.g., Venice), with emphasis on the cities' importance in the spread of Renaissance ideas.

3. Understand the effects of the reopening of the ancient "Silk Road" between Europe and China, including Marco Polo's travels and the location of his routes.

4. Describe the growth and effects of new ways of disseminating information (e.g., the ability to manufacture paper, translation of the Bible into the vernacular, printing).

5. Detail advances made in literature, the arts, science, mathematics, cartography, engineering, and the understanding of human anatomy and astronomy (e.g., by Dante Alighieri, Leonardo da Vinci, Michelangelo di Buonarroti Simoni, Johann Gutenberg, William Shakespeare).

7.9 Students analyze the historical developments of the Reformation.

1. List the causes for the internal turmoil in and weakening of the Catholic church (e.g., tax policies, selling of indulgences).

2. Describe the theological, political, and economic ideas of the major figures during the Reformation (e.g., Desiderius Erasmus, Martin Luther, John Calvin, William Tyndale).

3. Explain Protestants' new practices of church self-government and the influence of those practices on the development of democratic practices and ideas of federalism.

4. Identify and locate the European regions that remained Catholic and those that became Protestant and explain how the division affected the distribution of religions in the New World.

5. Analyze how the Counter-Reformation revitalized the Catholic church and the forces that fostered the movement (e.g., St. Ignatius of Loyola and the Jesuits, the Council of Trent).

6. Understand the institution and impact of missionaries on Christianity and the diffusion of Christianity from Europe to other parts of the world in the medieval and early modern periods; locate missions on a world map.

7. Describe the Golden Age of cooperation between Jews and Muslims in medieval Spain that promoted creativity in art, literature, and science, including how that cooperation was terminated by the religious persecution of individuals and groups (e.g., the Spanish Inquisition and the expulsion of Jews and Muslims from Spain in 1492).

7.10 Students analyze the historical developments of the Scientific Revolution and its lasting effect on religious, political, and cultural institutions.

1. Discuss the roots of the Scientific Revolution (e.g., Greek rationalism; Jewish, Christian, and Muslim science; Renaissance humanism; new knowledge from global exploration).

2. Understand the significance of the new scientific theories (e.g., those of Copernicus, Galileo, Kepler, Newton) and the significance of new inventions (e.g., the telescope, microscope, thermometer, barometer).

3. Understand the scientific method advanced by Bacon and Descartes, the influence of new scientific rationalism on the growth of democratic ideas, and the coexistence of science with traditional religious beliefs.

7.11 Students analyze political and economic change in the sixteenth, seventeenth, and eighteenth centuries (the Age of Exploration, the Enlightenment, and the Age of Reason).

1. Know the great voyages of discovery, the locations of the routes, and the influence of cartography in the development of a new European worldview.

2. Discuss the exchanges of plants, animals, technology, culture, and ideas among Europe, Africa, Asia, and the Americas in the fifteenth and sixteenth centuries and the major economic and social effects on each continent.

3. Examine the origins of modern capitalism; the influence of mercantilism and cottage industry; the elements and importance of a market economy in seventeenth-century Europe; the changing international trading and marketing patterns, including their locations on a world map; and the influence of explorers and map makers.

4. Explain how the main ideas of the Enlightenment can be traced back to such movements as the Renaissance, the Reformation, and the Scientific Revolution and to the Greeks, Romans, and Christianity.

5. Describe how democratic thought and institutions were influenced by Enlightenment thinkers (e.g., John Locke, Charles-Louis Montesquieu, American founders).

6. Discuss how the principles in the Magna Carta were embodied in such documents as the English Bill of Rights and the American Declaration of Independence.

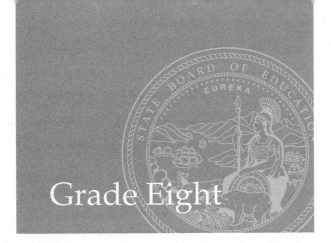

Grade Eight

United States History and Geography: Growth and Conflict

Students in grade eight study the ideas, issues, and events from the framing of the Constitution up to World War I, with an emphasis on America's role in the war. After reviewing the development of America's democratic institutions founded on the Judeo-Christian heritage and English parliamentary traditions, particularly the shaping of the Constitution, students trace the development of American politics, society, culture, and economy and relate them to the emergence of major regional differences. They learn about the challenges facing the new nation, with an emphasis on the causes, course, and consequences of the Civil War. They make connections between the rise of industrialization and contemporary social and economic conditions.

8.1 Students understand the major events preceding the founding of the nation and relate their significance to the development of American constitutional democracy.

1. Describe the relationship between the moral and political ideas of the Great Awakening and the development of revolutionary fervor.

2. Analyze the philosophy of government expressed in the Declaration of Independence, with an emphasis on government as a means of securing individual rights (e.g., key phrases such as "all men are created equal, that they are endowed by their Creator with certain unalienable Rights").

3. Analyze how the American Revolution affected other nations, especially France.

4. Describe the nation's blend of civic republicanism, classical liberal principles, and English parliamentary traditions.

8.2 Students analyze the political principles underlying the U.S. Constitution and compare the enumerated and implied powers of the federal government.

1. Discuss the significance of the Magna Carta, the English Bill of Rights, and the Mayflower Compact.

2. Analyze the Articles of Confederation and the Constitution and the success of each in implementing the ideals of the Declaration of Independence.

3. Evaluate the major debates that occurred during the development of the Constitution and their ultimate resolutions in such areas as shared power among institutions, divided state-federal power, slavery, the rights of individuals and states (later addressed by the addition of the Bill of Rights), and the status of American Indian nations under the commerce clause.

4. Describe the political philosophy underpinning the Constitution as specified in the *Federalist Papers* (authored by James Madison, Alexander Hamilton, and John Jay) and the role of such leaders as Madison, George Washington, Roger Sherman, Gouverneur Morris, and James Wilson in the writing and ratification of the Constitution.

5. Understand the significance of Jefferson's Statute for Religious Freedom as a forerunner of the First Amendment and the origins, purpose, and differing views of the founding fathers on the issue of the separation of church and state.

6. Enumerate the powers of government set forth in the Constitution and the fundamental liberties ensured by the Bill of Rights.

7. Describe the principles of federalism, dual sovereignty, separation of powers, checks and balances, the nature and purpose of majority rule, and the ways in which the American idea of constitutionalism preserves individual rights.

8.3 Students understand the foundation of the American political system and the ways in which citizens participate in it.

1. Analyze the principles and concepts codified in state constitutions between 1777 and 1781 that created the context out of which American political institutions and ideas developed.

2. Explain how the ordinances of 1785 and 1787 privatized national resources and transferred federally owned lands into private holdings, townships, and states.

3. Enumerate the advantages of a common market among the states as foreseen in and protected by the Constitution's clauses on interstate commerce, common coinage, and full-faith and credit.

4. Understand how the conflicts between Thomas Jefferson and Alexander Hamilton resulted in the emergence of two political parties (e.g., view of foreign policy, Alien and Sedition Acts, economic policy, National Bank, funding and assumption of the revolutionary debt).

5. Know the significance of domestic resistance movements and ways in which the central government responded to such movements (e.g., Shays' Rebellion, the Whiskey Rebellion).

6. Describe the basic law-making process and how the Constitution provides numerous opportunities for citizens to participate in the political process and to monitor and influence government (e.g., function of elections, political parties, interest groups).

7. Understand the functions and responsibilities of a free press.

8.4 Students analyze the aspirations and ideals of the people of the new nation.

1. Describe the country's physical landscapes, political divisions, and territorial expansion during the terms of the first four presidents.

2. Explain the policy significance of famous speeches (e.g., Washington's Farewell Address, Jefferson's 1801 Inaugural Address, John Q. Adams's Fourth of July 1821 Address).

3. Analyze the rise of capitalism and the economic problems and conflicts that accompanied it (e.g., Jackson's opposition to the National Bank; early decisions of the U.S. Supreme Court that reinforced the sanctity of contracts and a capitalist economic system of law).

4. Discuss daily life, including traditions in art, music, and literature, of early national America (e.g., through writings by Washington Irving, James Fenimore Cooper).

8.5 Students analyze U.S. foreign policy in the early Republic.

1. Understand the political and economic causes and consequences of the War of 1812 and know the major battles, leaders, and events that led to a final peace.

2. Know the changing boundaries of the United States and describe the relationships the country had with its neighbors (current Mexico and Canada) and Europe, including the influence of the Monroe Doctrine, and how those relationships influenced westward expansion and the Mexican-American War.

3. Outline the major treaties with American Indian nations during the administrations of the first four presidents and the varying outcomes of those treaties.

8.6 Students analyze the divergent paths of the American people from 1800 to the mid-1800s and the challenges they faced, with emphasis on the Northeast.

1. Discuss the influence of industrialization and technological developments on the region, including human modification of the landscape and how physical geography shaped human actions (e.g., growth of cities, deforestation, farming, mineral extraction).

2. Outline the physical obstacles to and the economic and political factors involved in building a network of roads, canals, and railroads (e.g., Henry Clay's American System).

3. List the reasons for the wave of immigration from Northern Europe to the United States and describe the growth in the number, size, and spatial arrangements of cities (e.g., Irish immigrants and the Great Irish Famine).

4. Study the lives of black Americans who gained freedom in the North and founded schools and churches to advance their rights and communities.

5. Trace the development of the American education system from its earliest roots, including the roles of religious and private schools and Horace Mann's campaign for free public education and its assimilating role in American culture.

6. Examine the women's suffrage movement (e.g., biographies, writings, and speeches of Elizabeth Cady Stanton, Margaret Fuller, Lucretia Mott, Susan B. Anthony).

7. Identify common themes in American art as well as transcendentalism and individualism (e.g., writings about and by Ralph Waldo Emerson, Henry David Thoreau, Herman Melville, Louisa May Alcott, Nathaniel Hawthorne, Henry Wadsworth Longfellow).

8.7   Students analyze the divergent paths of the American people in the South from 1800 to the mid-1800s and the challenges they faced.

1. Describe the development of the agrarian economy in the South, identify the locations of the cotton-producing states, and discuss the significance of cotton and the cotton gin.

2. Trace the origins and development of slavery; its effects on black Americans and on the region's political, social, religious, economic, and cultural development; and identify the strategies that were tried to both overturn and preserve it (e.g., through the writings and historical documents on Nat Turner, Denmark Vesey).

3. Examine the characteristics of white Southern society and how the physical environment influenced events and conditions prior to the Civil War.

4. Compare the lives of and opportunities for free blacks in the North with those of free blacks in the South.

8.8   Students analyze the divergent paths of the American people in the West from 1800 to the mid-1800s and the challenges they faced.

1. Discuss the election of Andrew Jackson as president in 1828, the importance of Jacksonian democracy, and his actions as president (e.g., the spoils system, veto of the National Bank, policy of Indian removal, opposition to the Supreme Court).

2. Describe the purpose, challenges, and economic incentives associated with westward expansion, including the concept of Manifest Destiny (e.g., the Lewis and Clark expedition, accounts of the removal of Indians, the Cherokees' "Trail of Tears," settlement of the Great Plains) and the territorial acquisitions that spanned numerous decades.

3. Describe the role of pioneer women and the new status that western women achieved (e.g., Laura Ingalls Wilder, Annie Bidwell; slave women gaining freedom in the West; Wyoming granting suffrage to women in 1869).

4. Examine the importance of the great rivers and the struggle over water rights.

5. Discuss Mexican settlements and their locations, cultural traditions, attitudes toward slavery, land-grant system, and economies.

6. Describe the Texas War for Independence and the Mexican-American War, including territorial settlements, the aftermath of the wars, and the effects the wars had on the lives of Americans, including Mexican Americans today.

8.9   Students analyze the early and steady attempts to abolish slavery and to realize the ideals of the Declaration of Independence.

1. Describe the leaders of the movement (e.g., John Quincy Adams and his proposed constitutional amendment, John Brown and the armed resistance, Harriet Tubman and the Underground Railroad, Benjamin Franklin, Theodore Weld, William Lloyd Garrison, Frederick Douglass).

2. Discuss the abolition of slavery in early state constitutions.

3. Describe the significance of the Northwest Ordinance in education and in the banning of slavery in new states north of the Ohio River.

4. Discuss the importance of the slavery issue as raised by the annexation of Texas and California's admission to the union as a free state under the Compromise of 1850.

5. Analyze the significance of the States' Rights Doctrine, the Missouri Compromise (1820), the Wilmot Proviso (1846), the Compromise of 1850, Henry Clay's role in the Missouri Compromise and the Compromise of 1850, the Kansas-Nebraska Act (1854), the *Dred Scott* v. *Sandford* decision (1857), and the Lincoln-Douglas debates (1858).

6. Describe the lives of free blacks and the laws that limited their freedom and economic opportunities.

8.10   Students analyze the multiple causes, key events, and complex consequences of the Civil War.

1. Compare the conflicting interpretations of state and federal authority as emphasized in the speeches and writings of statesmen such as Daniel Webster and John C. Calhoun.

2. Trace the boundaries constituting the North and the South, the geographical differences between the two regions, and the differences between agrarians and industrialists.

3. Identify the constitutional issues posed by the doctrine of nullification and secession and the earliest origins of that doctrine.

4. Discuss Abraham Lincoln's presidency and his significant writings and speeches and their relationship to the Declaration of Independence, such as his "House Divided" speech (1858), Gettysburg Address (1863), Emancipation Proclamation (1863), and inaugural addresses (1861 and 1865).

5. Study the views and lives of leaders (e.g., Ulysses S. Grant, Jefferson Davis, Robert E. Lee) and soldiers on both sides of the war, including those of black soldiers and regiments.

6. Describe critical developments and events in the war, including the major battles, geographical advantages and obstacles, technological advances, and General Lee's surrender at Appomattox.

7. Explain how the war affected combatants, civilians, the physical environment, and future warfare.

8.11 Students analyze the character and lasting consequences of Reconstruction.

1. List the original aims of Reconstruction and describe its effects on the political and social structures of different regions.

2. Identify the push-pull factors in the movement of former slaves to the cities in the North and to the West and their differing experiences in those regions (e.g., the experiences of Buffalo Soldiers).

3. Understand the effects of the Freedmen's Bureau and the restrictions placed on the rights and opportunities of freedmen, including racial segregation and "Jim Crow" laws.

4. Trace the rise of the Ku Klux Klan and describe the Klan's effects.

5. Understand the Thirteenth, Fourteenth, and Fifteenth Amendments to the Constitution and analyze their connection to Reconstruction.

8.12 Students analyze the transformation of the American economy and the changing social and political conditions in the United States in response to the Industrial Revolution.

1. Trace patterns of agricultural and industrial development as they relate to climate, use of natural resources, markets, and trade and locate such development on a map.

2. Identify the reasons for the development of federal Indian policy and the wars with American Indians and their relationship to agricultural development and industrialization.

3. Explain how states and the federal government encouraged business expansion through tariffs, banking, land grants, and subsidies.

4. Discuss entrepreneurs, industrialists, and bankers in politics, commerce, and industry (e.g., Andrew Carnegie, John D. Rockefeller, Leland Stanford).

5. Examine the location and effects of urbanization, renewed immigration, and industrialization (e.g., the effects on social fabric of cities, wealth and economic opportunity, the conservation movement).

6. Discuss child labor, working conditions, and laissez-faire policies toward big business and examine the labor movement, including its leaders (e.g., Samuel Gompers), its demand for collective bargaining, and its strikes and protests over labor conditions.

7. Identify the new sources of large-scale immigration and the contributions of immigrants to the building of cities and the economy; explain the ways in which new social and economic patterns encouraged assimilation of newcomers into the mainstream amidst growing cultural diversity; and discuss the new wave of nativism.

8. Identify the characteristics and impact of Grangerism and Populism.

9. Name the significant inventors and their inventions and identify how they improved the quality of life (e.g., Thomas Edison, Alexander Graham Bell, Orville and Wilbur Wright).

Historical and Social Sciences Analysis Skills

The intellectual skills noted below are to be learned through, and applied to, the content standards for grades nine through twelve. They are to be assessed *only in conjunction with* the content standards in grades nine through twelve.

In addition to the standards for grades nine through twelve, students demonstrate the following intellectual, reasoning, reflection, and research skills.

Chronological and Spatial Thinking

1. Students compare the present with the past, evaluating the consequences of past events and decisions and determining the lessons that were learned.

2. Students analyze how change happens at different rates at different times; understand that some aspects can change while others remain the same; and understand that change is complicated and affects not only technology and politics but also values and beliefs.

3. Students use a variety of maps and documents to interpret human movement, including major patterns of domestic and international migration, changing environmental preferences and settlement patterns, the frictions that develop between population groups, and the diffusion of ideas, technological innovations, and goods.

4. Students relate current events to the physical and human characteristics of places and regions.

Historical Research, Evidence, and Point of View

1. Students distinguish valid arguments from fallacious arguments in historical interpretations.

2. Students identify bias and prejudice in historical interpretations.

3. Students evaluate major debates among historians concerning alternative interpretations of the past, including an analysis of authors' use of evidence and the distinctions between sound generalizations and misleading oversimplifications.

4. Students construct and test hypotheses; collect, evaluate, and employ information from multiple primary and secondary sources; and apply it in oral and written presentations.

Historical Interpretation

1. Students show the connections, causal and otherwise, between particular historical events and larger social, economic, and political trends and developments.

2. Students recognize the complexity of historical causes and effects, including the limitations on determining cause and effect.

3. Students interpret past events and issues within the context in which an event unfolded rather than solely in terms of present-day norms and values.

4. Students understand the meaning, implication, and impact of historical events and recognize that events could have taken other directions.

5. Students analyze human modifications of landscapes and examine the resulting environmental policy issues.

6. Students conduct cost-benefit analyses and apply basic economic indicators to analyze the aggregate economic behavior of the U.S. economy.

World History, Culture, and Geography: The Modern World

Students in grade ten study major turning points that shaped the modern world, from the late eighteenth century through the present, including the cause and course of the two world wars. They trace the rise of democratic ideas and develop an understanding of the historical roots of current world issues, especially as they pertain to international relations. They extrapolate from the American experience that democratic ideals are often achieved at a high price, remain vulnerable, and are not practiced everywhere in the world. Students develop an understanding of current world issues and relate them to their historical, geographic, political, economic, and cultural contexts. Students consider multiple accounts of events in order to understand international relations from a variety of perspectives.

10.1 **Students relate the moral and ethical principles in ancient Greek and Roman philosophy, in Judaism, and in Christianity to the development of Western political thought.**

1. Analyze the similarities and differences in Judeo-Christian and Greco-Roman views of law, reason and faith, and duties of the individual.

2. Trace the development of the Western political ideas of the rule of law and illegitimacy of tyranny, using selections from Plato's *Republic* and Aristotle's *Politics*.

3. Consider the influence of the U.S. Constitution on political systems in the contemporary world.

10.2 **Students compare and contrast the Glorious Revolution of England, the American Revolution, and the French Revolution and their enduring effects worldwide on the political expectations for self-government and individual liberty.**

1. Compare the major ideas of philosophers and their effects on the democratic revolutions in England, the United States, France, and Latin America (e.g., John Locke,

Charles-Louis Montesquieu, Jean-Jacques Rousseau, Simón Bolívar, Thomas Jefferson, James Madison).

2. List the principles of the Magna Carta, the English Bill of Rights (1689), the American Declaration of Independence (1776), the French Declaration of the Rights of Man and the Citizen (1789), and the U.S. Bill of Rights (1791).

3. Understand the unique character of the American Revolution, its spread to other parts of the world, and its continuing significance to other nations.

4. Explain how the ideology of the French Revolution led France to develop from constitutional monarchy to democratic despotism to the Napoleonic empire.

5. Discuss how nationalism spread across Europe with Napoleon but was repressed for a generation under the Congress of Vienna and Concert of Europe until the Revolutions of 1848.

10.3   Students analyze the effects of the Industrial Revolution in England, France, Germany, Japan, and the United States.

1. Analyze why England was the first country to industrialize.

2. Examine how scientific and technological changes and new forms of energy brought about massive social, economic, and cultural change (e.g., the inventions and discoveries of James Watt, Eli Whitney, Henry Bessemer, Louis Pasteur, Thomas Edison).

3. Describe the growth of population, rural to urban migration, and growth of cities associated with the Industrial Revolution.

4. Trace the evolution of work and labor, including the demise of the slave trade and the effects of immigration, mining and manufacturing, division of labor, and the union movement.

5. Understand the connections among natural resources, entrepreneurship, labor, and capital in an industrial economy.

6. Analyze the emergence of capitalism as a dominant economic pattern and the responses to it, including Utopianism, Social Democracy, Socialism, and Communism.

7. Describe the emergence of Romanticism in art and literature (e.g., the poetry of William Blake and William Wordsworth), social criticism (e.g., the novels of Charles Dickens), and the move away from Classicism in Europe.

10.4   Students analyze patterns of global change in the era of New Imperialism in at least two of the following regions or countries: Africa, Southeast Asia, China, India, Latin America, and the Philippines.

1. Describe the rise of industrial economies and their link to imperialism and colonialism (e.g., the role played by national security and strategic advantage; moral issues raised by the search for national hegemony, Social Darwinism, and the missionary impulse; material issues such as land, resources, and technology).

2. Discuss the locations of the colonial rule of such nations as England, France, Germany, Italy, Japan, the Netherlands, Russia, Spain, Portugal, and the United States.

3. Explain imperialism from the perspective of the colonizers and the colonized and the varied immediate and long-term responses by the people under colonial rule.

4. Describe the independence struggles of the colonized regions of the world, including the roles of leaders, such as Sun Yat-sen in China, and the roles of ideology and religion.

10.5   Students analyze the causes and course of the First World War.

1. Analyze the arguments for entering into war presented by leaders from all sides of the Great War and the role of political and economic rivalries, ethnic and ideological conflicts, domestic discontent and disorder, and propaganda and nationalism in mobilizing the civilian population in support of "total war."

2. Examine the principal theaters of battle, major turning points, and the importance of geographic factors in military decisions and outcomes (e.g., topography, waterways, distance, climate).

3. Explain how the Russian Revolution and the entry of the United States affected the course and outcome of the war.

4. Understand the nature of the war and its human costs (military and civilian) on all sides of the conflict, including how colonial peoples contributed to the war effort.

5. Discuss human rights violations and genocide, including the Ottoman government's actions against Armenian citizens.

10.6   Students analyze the effects of the First World War.

1. Analyze the aims and negotiating roles of world leaders, the terms and influence of the Treaty of Versailles and Woodrow Wilson's Fourteen Points, and the causes and effects of the United States's rejection of the League of Nations on world politics.

2. Describe the effects of the war and resulting peace treaties on population movement, the international economy, and shifts in the geographic and political borders of Europe and the Middle East.

3. Understand the widespread disillusionment with prewar institutions, authorities, and values that resulted in a void that was later filled by totalitarians.

4. Discuss the influence of World War I on literature, art, and intellectual life in the West (e.g., Pablo Picasso, the "lost generation" of Gertrude Stein, Ernest Hemingway).

10.7   Students analyze the rise of totalitarian governments after World War I.

1. Understand the causes and consequences of the Russian Revolution, including Lenin's use of totalitarian means to seize and maintain control (e.g., the Gulag).

2. Trace Stalin's rise to power in the Soviet Union and the connection between economic policies, political policies, the absence of a free press, and systematic violations of human rights (e.g., the Terror Famine in Ukraine).

3. Analyze the rise, aggression, and human costs of totalitarian regimes (Fascist and Communist) in Germany, Italy, and the Soviet Union, noting especially their common and dissimilar traits.

10.8   Students analyze the causes and consequences of World War II.

1. Compare the German, Italian, and Japanese drives for empire in the 1930s, including the 1937 Rape of Nanking, other atrocities in China, and the Stalin-Hitler Pact of 1939.

2. Understand the role of appeasement, nonintervention (isolationism), and the domestic distractions in Europe and the United States prior to the outbreak of World War II.

3. Identify and locate the Allied and Axis powers on a map and discuss the major turning points of the war, the principal theaters of conflict, key strategic decisions, and the resulting war conferences and political resolutions, with emphasis on the importance of geographic factors.

4. Describe the political, diplomatic, and military leaders during the war (e.g., Winston Churchill, Franklin Delano Roosevelt, Emperor Hirohito, Adolf Hitler, Benito Mussolini, Joseph Stalin, Douglas MacArthur, Dwight Eisenhower).

5. Analyze the Nazi policy of pursuing racial purity, especially against the European Jews; its transformation into the Final Solution; and the Holocaust that resulted in the murder of six million Jewish civilians.

6. Discuss the human costs of the war, with particular attention to the civilian and military losses in Russia, Germany, Britain, the United States, China, and Japan.

10.9   Students analyze the international developments in the post–World War II world.

1. Compare the economic and military power shifts caused by the war, including the Yalta Pact, the development of nuclear weapons, Soviet control over Eastern European nations, and the economic recoveries of Germany and Japan.

2. Analyze the causes of the Cold War, with the free world on one side and Soviet client states on the other, including competition for influence in such places as Egypt, the Congo, Vietnam, and Chile.

3. Understand the importance of the Truman Doctrine and the Marshall Plan, which established the pattern for America's postwar policy of supplying economic and military aid to prevent the spread of Communism and the resulting economic and political competition in arenas such as Southeast Asia (i.e., the Korean War, Vietnam War), Cuba, and Africa.

4. Analyze the Chinese Civil War, the rise of Mao Tse-tung, and the subsequent political and economic upheavals in China (e.g., the Great Leap Forward, the Cultural Revolution, and the Tiananmen Square uprising).

5. Describe the uprisings in Poland (1952), Hungary (1956), and Czechoslovakia (1968) and those countries' resurgence in the 1970s and 1980s as people in Soviet satellites sought freedom from Soviet control.

6. Understand how the forces of nationalism developed in the Middle East, how the Holocaust affected world opinion regarding the need for a Jewish state, and the significance and effects of the location and establishment of Israel on world affairs.

7. Analyze the reasons for the collapse of the Soviet Union, including the weakness of the command economy, burdens of military commitments, and growing resistance to Soviet rule by dissidents in satellite states and the non-Russian Soviet republics.

8. Discuss the establishment and work of the United Nations and the purposes and functions of the Warsaw Pact, SEATO, NATO, and the Organization of American States.

10.10 Students analyze instances of nation-building in the contemporary world in at least two of the following regions or countries: the Middle East, Africa, Mexico and other parts of Latin America, and China.

1. Understand the challenges in the regions, including their geopolitical, cultural, military, and economic significance and the international relationships in which they are involved.

2. Describe the recent history of the regions, including political divisions and systems, key leaders, religious issues, natural features, resources, and population patterns.

3. Discuss the important trends in the regions today and whether they appear to serve the cause of individual freedom and democracy.

10.11 Students analyze the integration of countries into the world economy and the information, technological, and communications revolutions (e.g., television, satellites, computers).

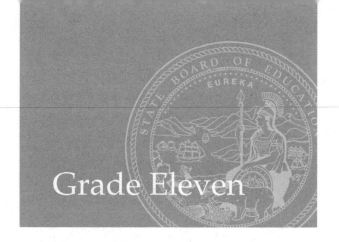

Grade Eleven

United States History and Geography: Continuity and Change in the Twentieth Century

Students in grade eleven study the major turning points in American history in the twentieth century. Following a review of the nation's beginnings and the impact of the Enlightenment on U.S. democratic ideals, students build upon the tenth grade study of global industrialization to understand the emergence and impact of new technology and a corporate economy, including the social and cultural effects. They trace the change in the ethnic composition of American society; the movement toward equal rights for racial minorities and women; and the role of the United States as a major world power. An emphasis is placed on the expanding role of the federal government and federal courts as well as the continuing tension between the individual and the state. Students consider the major social problems of our time and trace their causes in historical events. They learn that the United States has served as a model for other nations and that the rights and freedoms we enjoy are not accidents, but the results of a defined set of political principles that are not always basic to citizens of other countries. Students understand that our rights under the U.S. Constitution are a precious inheritance that depends on an educated citizenry for their preservation and protection.

11.1   Students analyze the significant events in the founding of the nation and its attempts to realize the philosophy of government described in the Declaration of Independence.

1. Describe the Enlightenment and the rise of democratic ideas as the context in which the nation was founded.

2. Analyze the ideological origins of the American Revolution, the Founding Fathers' philosophy of divinely bestowed unalienable natural rights, the debates on the drafting and ratification of the Constitution, and the addition of the Bill of Rights.

3. Understand the history of the Constitution after 1787 with emphasis on federal versus state authority and growing democratization.

4. Examine the effects of the Civil War and Reconstruction and of the industrial revolution, including demographic shifts and the emergence in the late nineteenth century of the United States as a world power.

11.2   Students analyze the relationship among the rise of industrialization, large-scale rural-to-urban migration, and massive immigration from Southern and Eastern Europe.

1. Know the effects of industrialization on living and working conditions, including the portrayal of working conditions and food safety in Upton Sinclair's *The Jungle*.

2. Describe the changing landscape, including the growth of cities linked by industry and trade, and the development of cities divided according to race, ethnicity, and class.

3. Trace the effect of the Americanization movement.

4. Analyze the effect of urban political machines and responses to them by immigrants and middle-class reformers.

5. Discuss corporate mergers that produced trusts and cartels and the economic and political policies of industrial leaders.

6. Trace the economic development of the United States and its emergence as a major industrial power, including its gains from trade and the advantages of its physical geography.

7. Analyze the similarities and differences between the ideologies of Social Darwinism and Social Gospel (e.g., using biographies of William Graham Sumner, Billy Sunday, Dwight L. Moody).

8. Examine the effect of political programs and activities of Populists.

9. Understand the effect of political programs and activities of the Progressives (e.g., federal regulation of railroad transport, Children's Bureau, the Sixteenth Amendment, Theodore Roosevelt, Hiram Johnson).

11.3   Students analyze the role religion played in the founding of America, its lasting moral, social, and political impacts, and issues regarding religious liberty.

1. Describe the contributions of various religious groups to American civic principles and social reform movements (e.g., civil and human rights, individual responsibility and the work ethic, antimonarchy and self-rule, worker protection, family-centered communities).

2. Analyze the great religious revivals and the leaders involved in them, including the First Great Awakening, the Second Great Awakening, the Civil War revivals, the Social Gospel Movement, the rise of Christian liberal theology in the nineteenth century, the impact of the Second Vatican Council, and the rise of Christian fundamentalism in current times.

3. Cite incidences of religious intolerance in the United States (e.g., persecution of Mormons, anti-Catholic sentiment, anti-Semitism).

4. Discuss the expanding religious pluralism in the United States and California that resulted from large-scale immigration in the twentieth century.

5. Describe the principles of religious liberty found in the Establishment and Free Exercise clauses of the First Amendment, including the debate on the issue of separation of church and state.

11.4   Students trace the rise of the United States to its role as a world power in the twentieth century.

1. List the purpose and the effects of the Open Door policy.

2. Describe the Spanish-American War and U.S. expansion in the South Pacific.

3. Discuss America's role in the Panama Revolution and the building of the Panama Canal.

4. Explain Theodore Roosevelt's Big Stick diplomacy, William Taft's Dollar Diplomacy, and Woodrow Wilson's Moral Diplomacy, drawing on relevant speeches.

5. Analyze the political, economic, and social ramifications of World War I on the home front.

6. Trace the declining role of Great Britain and the expanding role of the United States in world affairs after World War II.

11.5   Students analyze the major political, social, economic, technological, and cultural developments of the 1920s.

1. Discuss the policies of Presidents Warren Harding, Calvin Coolidge, and Herbert Hoover.

2. Analyze the international and domestic events, interests, and philosophies that prompted attacks on civil liberties, including the Palmer Raids, Marcus Garvey's "back-to-Africa" movement, the Ku Klux Klan, and immigration quotas and the responses of organizations such as the American Civil Liberties Union, the National Association for the Advancement of Colored People, and the Anti-Defamation League to those attacks.

3. Examine the passage of the Eighteenth Amendment to the Constitution and the Volstead Act (Prohibition).

4. Analyze the passage of the Nineteenth Amendment and the changing role of women in society.

5. Describe the Harlem Renaissance and new trends in literature, music, and art, with special attention to the work of writers (e.g., Zora Neale Hurston, Langston Hughes).

6. Trace the growth and effects of radio and movies and their role in the worldwide diffusion of popular culture.

7. Discuss the rise of mass production techniques, the growth of cities, the impact of new technologies (e.g., the automobile, electricity), and the resulting prosperity and effect on the American landscape.

11.6 Students analyze the different explanations for the Great Depression and how the New Deal fundamentally changed the role of the federal government.

1. Describe the monetary issues of the late nineteenth and early twentieth centuries that gave rise to the establishment of the Federal Reserve and the weaknesses in key sectors of the economy in the late 1920s.

2. Understand the explanations of the principal causes of the Great Depression and the steps taken by the Federal Reserve, Congress, and Presidents Herbert Hoover and Franklin Delano Roosevelt to combat the economic crisis.

3. Discuss the human toll of the Depression, natural disasters, and unwise agricultural practices and their effects on the depopulation of rural regions and on political movements of the left and right, with particular attention to the Dust Bowl refugees and their social and economic impacts in California.

4. Analyze the effects of and the controversies arising from New Deal economic policies and the expanded role of the federal government in society and the economy since the 1930s (e.g., Works Progress Administration, Social Security, National Labor Relations Board, farm programs, regional development policies, and energy development projects such as the Tennessee Valley Authority, California Central Valley Project, and Bonneville Dam).

5. Trace the advances and retreats of organized labor, from the creation of the American Federation of Labor and the Congress of Industrial Organizations to current issues of a postindustrial, multinational economy, including the United Farm Workers in California.

11.7 Students analyze America's participation in World War II.

1. Examine the origins of American involvement in the war, with an emphasis on the events that precipitated the attack on Pearl Harbor.

2. Explain U.S. and Allied wartime strategy, including the major battles of Midway, Normandy, Iwo Jima, Okinawa, and the Battle of the Bulge.

3. Identify the roles and sacrifices of individual American soldiers, as well as the unique contributions of the special fighting forces (e.g., the Tuskegee Airmen, the 442nd Regimental Combat team, the Navajo Code Talkers).

4. Analyze Roosevelt's foreign policy during World War II (e.g., Four Freedoms speech).

5. Discuss the constitutional issues and impact of events on the U.S. home front, including the internment of Japanese Americans (e.g., *Fred Korematsu* v. *United States of*

America) and the restrictions on German and Italian resident aliens; the response of the administration to Hitler's atrocities against Jews and other groups; the roles of women in military production; and the roles and growing political demands of African Americans.

6. Describe major developments in aviation, weaponry, communication, and medicine and the war's impact on the location of American industry and use of resources.

7. Discuss the decision to drop atomic bombs and the consequences of the decision (Hiroshima and Nagasaki).

8. Analyze the effect of massive aid given to Western Europe under the Marshall Plan to rebuild itself after the war and the importance of a rebuilt Europe to the U.S. economy.

11.8 Students analyze the economic boom and social transformation of post–World War II America.

1. Trace the growth of service sector, white collar, and professional sector jobs in business and government.

2. Describe the significance of Mexican immigration and its relationship to the agricultural economy, especially in California.

3. Examine Truman's labor policy and congressional reaction to it.

4. Analyze new federal government spending on defense, welfare, interest on the national debt, and federal and state spending on education, including the California Master Plan.

5. Describe the increased powers of the presidency in response to the Great Depression, World War II, and the Cold War.

6. Discuss the diverse environmental regions of North America, their relationship to local economies, and the origins and prospects of environmental problems in those regions.

7. Describe the effects on society and the economy of technological developments since 1945, including the computer revolution, changes in communication, advances in medicine, and improvements in agricultural technology.

8. Discuss forms of popular culture, with emphasis on their origins and geographic diffusion (e.g., jazz and other forms of popular music, professional sports, architectural and artistic styles).

11.9 Students analyze U.S. foreign policy since World War II.

1. Discuss the establishment of the United Nations and International Declaration of Human Rights, International Monetary Fund, World Bank, and General Agreement on Tariffs and Trade (GATT) and their importance in shaping modern Europe and maintaining peace and international order.

2. Understand the role of military alliances, including NATO and SEATO, in deterring communist aggression and maintaining security during the Cold War.

3. Trace the origins and geopolitical consequences (foreign and domestic) of the Cold War and containment policy, including the following:

   • The era of McCarthyism, instances of domestic Communism (e.g., Alger Hiss) and blacklisting

   • The Truman Doctrine

   • The Berlin Blockade

   • The Korean War

   • The Bay of Pigs invasion and the Cuban Missile Crisis

   • Atomic testing in the American West, the "mutual assured destruction" doctrine, and disarmament policies

   • The Vietnam War

   • Latin American policy

4. List the effects of foreign policy on domestic policies and vice versa (e.g., protests during the war in Vietnam, the "nuclear freeze" movement).

5. Analyze the role of the Reagan administration and other factors in the victory of the West in the Cold War.

6. Describe U.S. Middle East policy and its strategic, political, and economic interests, including those related to the Gulf War.

7. Examine relations between the United States and Mexico in the twentieth century, including key economic, political, immigration, and environmental issues.

11.10 Students analyze the development of federal civil rights and voting rights.

1. Explain how demands of African Americans helped produce a stimulus for civil rights, including President Roosevelt's ban on racial discrimination in defense industries in 1941, and how African Americans' service in World War II produced a stimulus for President Truman's decision to end segregation in the armed forces in 1948.

2. Examine and analyze the key events, policies, and court cases in the evolution of civil rights, including *Dred Scott* v. *Sandford, Plessy* v. *Ferguson, Brown* v. *Board of Education, Regents of the University of California* v. *Bakke,* and California Proposition 209.

3. Describe the collaboration on legal strategy between African American and white civil rights lawyers to end racial segregation in higher education.

4. Examine the roles of civil rights advocates (e.g., A. Philip Randolph, Martin Luther King, Jr., Malcom X, Thurgood Marshall, James Farmer, Rosa Parks), including the significance of Martin Luther King, Jr.'s "Letter from Birmingham Jail" and "I Have a Dream" speech.

5. Discuss the diffusion of the civil rights movement of African Americans from the churches of the rural South and the urban North, including the resistance to racial desegregation in Little Rock and Birmingham, and how the advances influenced the agendas, strategies, and effectiveness of the quests of American Indians, Asian Americans, and Hispanic Americans for civil rights and equal opportunities.

6. Analyze the passage and effects of civil rights and voting rights legislation (e.g., 1964 Civil Rights Act, Voting Rights Act of 1965) and the Twenty-Fourth Amendment, with an emphasis on equality of access to education and to the political process.

7. Analyze the women's rights movement from the era of Elizabeth Stanton and Susan Anthony and the passage of the Nineteenth Amendment to the movement launched in the 1960s, including differing perspectives on the roles of women.

11.11 Students analyze the major social problems and domestic policy issues in contemporary American society.

1. Discuss the reasons for the nation's changing immigration policy, with emphasis on how the Immigration Act of 1965 and successor acts have transformed American society.

2. Discuss the significant domestic policy speeches of Truman, Eisenhower, Kennedy,, Johnson, Nixon, Carter, Reagan, Bush, and Clinton (e.g., with regard to education, civil rights, economic policy, environmental policy).

3. Describe the changing roles of women in society as reflected in the entry of more women into the labor force and the changing family structure.

4. Explain the constitutional crisis originating from the Watergate scandal.

5. Trace the impact of, need for, and controversies associated with environmental conservation, expansion of the national park system, and the development of environmental protection laws, with particular attention to the interaction between environmental protection advocates and property rights advocates.

6. Analyze the persistence of poverty and how different analyses of this issue influence welfare reform, health insurance reform, and other social policies.

7. Explain how the federal, state, and local governments have responded to demographic and social changes such as population shifts to the suburbs, racial concentrations in the cities, Frostbelt-to-Sunbelt migration, international migration, decline of family farms, increases in out-of-wedlock births, and drug abuse.

Grade Twelve

Principles of American Democracy and Economics

Students in grade twelve pursue a deeper understanding of the institutions of American government. They compare systems of government in the world today and analyze the history and changing interpretations of the Constitution, the Bill of Rights, and the current state of the legislative, executive, and judiciary branches of government. An emphasis is placed on analyzing the relationship among federal, state, and local governments, with particular attention paid to important historical documents such as the *Federalist Papers*. These standards represent the culmination of civic literacy as students prepare to vote, participate in community activities, and assume the responsibilities of citizenship.

In addition to studying government in grade twelve, students will also master fundamental economic concepts, applying the tools (graphs, statistics, equations) from other subject areas to the understanding of operations and institutions of economic systems. Studied in a historic context are the basic economic principles of micro- and macroeconomics, international economics, comparative economic systems, measurement, and methods.

Principles of American Democracy

12.1 Students explain the fundamental principles and moral values of American democracy as expressed in the U.S. Constitution and other essential documents of American democracy.

1. Analyze the influence of ancient Greek, Roman, English, and leading European political thinkers such as John Locke, Charles-Louis Montesquieu, Niccolò Machiavelli, and William Blackstone on the development of American government.

2. Discuss the character of American democracy and its promise and perils as articulated by Alexis de Tocqueville.

3. Explain how the U.S. Constitution reflects a balance between the classical republican concern with promotion of the public good and the classical liberal concern with protecting individual rights; and discuss how the basic premises of liberal constitutionalism and democracy are joined in the Declaration of Independence as "self-evident truths."

4. Explain how the Founding Fathers' realistic view of human nature led directly to the establishment of a constitutional system that limited the power of the governors and the governed as articulated in the *Federalist Papers*.

5. Describe the systems of separated and shared powers, the role of organized interests (*Federalist Paper Number 10*), checks and balances (*Federalist Paper Number 51*), the importance of an independent judiciary (*Federalist Paper Number 78*), enumerated powers, rule of law, federalism, and civilian control of the military.

6. Understand that the Bill of Rights limits the powers of the federal government and state governments.

12.2   Students evaluate and take and defend positions on the scope and limits of rights and obligations as democratic citizens, the relationships among them, and how they are secured.

1. Discuss the meaning and importance of each of the rights guaranteed under the Bill of Rights and how each is secured (e.g., freedom of religion, speech, press, assembly, petition, privacy).

2. Explain how economic rights are secured and their importance to the individual and to society (e.g., the right to acquire, use, transfer, and dispose of property; right to choose one's work; right to join or not join labor unions; copyright and patent).

3. Discuss the individual's legal obligations to obey the law, serve as a juror, and pay taxes.

4. Understand the obligations of civic-mindedness, including voting, being informed on civic issues, volunteering and performing public service, and serving in the military or alternative service.

5. Describe the reciprocity between rights and obligations; that is, why enjoyment of one's rights entails respect for the rights of others.

6. Explain how one becomes a citizen of the United States, including the process of naturalization (e.g., literacy, language, and other requirements).

12.3   Students evaluate and take and defend positions on what the fundamental values and principles of civil society are (i.e., the autonomous sphere of voluntary personal, social, and economic relations that are not part of government), their interdependence, and the meaning and importance of those values and principles for a free society.

1. Explain how civil society provides opportunities for individuals to associate for social, cultural, religious, economic, and political purposes.

2. Explain how civil society makes it possible for people, individually or in association with others, to bring their influence to bear on government in ways other than voting and elections.

3. Discuss the historical role of religion and religious diversity.

4. Compare the relationship of government and civil society in constitutional democracies to the relationship of government and civil society in authoritarian and totalitarian regimes.

12.4 Students analyze the unique roles and responsibilities of the three branches of government as established by the U.S. Constitution.

1. Discuss Article I of the Constitution as it relates to the legislative branch, including eligibility for office and lengths of terms of representatives and senators; election to office; the roles of the House and Senate in impeachment proceedings; the role of the vice president; the enumerated legislative powers; and the process by which a bill becomes a law.

2. Explain the process through which the Constitution can be amended.

3. Identify their current representatives in the legislative branch of the national government.

4. Discuss Article II of the Constitution as it relates to the executive branch, including eligibility for office and length of term, election to and removal from office, the oath of office, and the enumerated executive powers.

5. Discuss Article III of the Constitution as it relates to judicial power, including the length of terms of judges and the jurisdiction of the Supreme Court.

6. Explain the processes of selection and confirmation of Supreme Court justices.

12.5 Students summarize landmark U.S. Supreme Court interpretations of the Constitution and its amendments.

1. Understand the changing interpretations of the Bill of Rights over time, including interpretations of the basic freedoms (religion, speech, press, petition, and assembly) articulated in the First Amendment and the due process and equal-protection-of-the-law clauses of the Fourteenth Amendment.

2. Analyze judicial activism and judicial restraint and the effects of each policy over the decades (e.g., the Warren and Rehnquist courts).

3. Evaluate the effects of the Court's interpretations of the Constitution in *Marbury* v. *Madison, McCulloch* v. *Maryland,* and *United States* v. *Nixon,* with emphasis on the arguments espoused by each side in these cases.

4. Explain the controversies that have resulted over changing interpretations of civil rights, including those in *Plessy* v. *Ferguson, Brown* v. *Board of Education, Miranda* v. *Arizona, Regents of the University of California* v. *Bakke, Adarand Constructors, Inc.* v. *Pena,* and *United States* v. *Virginia* (VMI).

12.6   Students evaluate issues regarding campaigns for national, state, and local elective offices.

1. Analyze the origin, development, and role of political parties, noting those occasional periods in which there was only one major party or were more than two major parties.

2. Discuss the history of the nomination process for presidential candidates and the increasing importance of primaries in general elections.

3. Evaluate the roles of polls, campaign advertising, and the controversies over campaign funding.

4. Describe the means that citizens use to participate in the political process (e.g., voting, campaigning, lobbying, filing a legal challenge, demonstrating, petitioning, picketing, running for political office).

5. Discuss the features of direct democracy in numerous states (e.g., the process of referendums, recall elections).

6. Analyze trends in voter turnout; the causes and effects of reapportionment and redistricting, with special attention to spatial districting and the rights of minorities; and the function of the Electoral College.

12.7   Students analyze and compare the powers and procedures of the national, state, tribal, and local governments.

1. Explain how conflicts between levels of government and branches of government are resolved.

2. Identify the major responsibilities and sources of revenue for state and local governments.

3. Discuss reserved powers and concurrent powers of state governments.

4. Discuss the Ninth and Tenth Amendments and interpretations of the extent of the federal government's power.

5. Explain how public policy is formed, including the setting of the public agenda and implementation of it through regulations and executive orders.

6. Compare the processes of lawmaking at each of the three levels of government, including the role of lobbying and the media.

7. Identify the organization and jurisdiction of federal, state, and local (e.g., California) courts and the interrelationships among them.

8. Understand the scope of presidential power and decision making through examination of case studies such as the Cuban Missile Crisis, passage of Great Society legislation, War Powers Act, Gulf War, and Bosnia.

12.8 Students evaluate and take and defend positions on the influence of the media on American political life.

1. Discuss the meaning and importance of a free and responsible press.

2. Describe the roles of broadcast, print, and electronic media, including the Internet, as means of communication in American politics.

3. Explain how public officials use the media to communicate with the citizenry and to shape public opinion.

12.9 Students analyze the origins, characteristics, and development of different political systems across time, with emphasis on the quest for political democracy, its advances, and its obstacles.

1. Explain how the different philosophies and structures of feudalism, mercantilism, socialism, fascism, communism, monarchies, parliamentary systems, and constitutional liberal democracies influence economic policies, social welfare policies, and human rights practices.

2. Compare the various ways in which power is distributed, shared, and limited in systems of shared powers and in parliamentary systems, including the influence and role of parliamentary leaders (e.g., William Gladstone, Margaret Thatcher).

3. Discuss the advantages and disadvantages of federal, confederal, and unitary systems of government.

4. Describe for at least two countries the consequences of conditions that gave rise to tyrannies during certain periods (e.g., Italy, Japan, Haiti, Nigeria, Cambodia).

5. Identify the forms of illegitimate power that twentieth-century African, Asian, and Latin American dictators used to gain and hold office and the conditions and interests that supported them.

6. Identify the ideologies, causes, stages, and outcomes of major Mexican, Central American, and South American revolutions in the nineteenth and twentieth centuries.

7. Describe the ideologies that give rise to Communism, methods of maintaining control, and the movements to overthrow such governments in Czechoslovakia, Hungary, and Poland, including the roles of individuals (e.g., Alexander Solzhenitsyn, Pope John Paul II, Lech Walesa, Vaclav Havel).

8. Identify the successes of relatively new democracies in Africa, Asia, and Latin America and the ideas, leaders, and general societal conditions that have launched and sustained, or failed to sustain, them.

12.10 Students formulate questions about and defend their analyses of tensions within our constitutional democracy and the importance of maintaining a balance between the following concepts: majority rule and individual rights; liberty and equality; state and national authority in a federal system; civil disobedience and the rule of law; freedom of the press and the right to a fair trial; the relationship of religion and government.

Principles of Economics

12.1 Students understand common economic terms and concepts and economic reasoning.

1. Examine the causal relationship between scarcity and the need for choices.
2. Explain opportunity cost and marginal benefit and marginal cost.
3. Identify the difference between monetary and nonmonetary incentives and how changes in incentives cause changes in behavior.
4. Evaluate the role of private property as an incentive in conserving and improving scarce resources, including renewable and nonrenewable natural resources.
5. Analyze the role of a market economy in establishing and preserving political and personal liberty (e.g., through the works of Adam Smith).

12.2 Students analyze the elements of America's market economy in a global setting.

1. Understand the relationship of the concept of incentives to the law of supply and the relationship of the concept of incentives and substitutes to the law of demand.
2. Discuss the effects of changes in supply and/or demand on the relative scarcity, price, and quantity of particular products.
3. Explain the roles of property rights, competition, and profit in a market economy.
4. Explain how prices reflect the relative scarcity of goods and services and perform the allocative function in a market economy.
5. Understand the process by which competition among buyers and sellers determines a market price.
6. Describe the effect of price controls on buyers and sellers.
7. Analyze how domestic and international competition in a market economy affects goods and services produced and the quality, quantity, and price of those products.
8. Explain the role of profit as the incentive to entrepreneurs in a market economy.

9. Describe the functions of the financial markets.

10. Discuss the economic principles that guide the location of agricultural production and industry and the spatial distribution of transportation and retail facilities.

12.3 Students analyze the influence of the federal government on the American economy.

1. Understand how the role of government in a market economy often includes providing for national defense, addressing environmental concerns, defining and enforcing property rights, attempting to make markets more competitive, and protecting consumers' rights.

2. Identify the factors that may cause the costs of government actions to outweigh the benefits.

3. Describe the aims of government fiscal policies (taxation, borrowing, spending) and their influence on production, employment, and price levels.

4. Understand the aims and tools of monetary policy and their influence on economic activity (e.g., the Federal Reserve).

12.4 Students analyze the elements of the U.S. labor market in a global setting.

1. Understand the operations of the labor market, including the circumstances surrounding the establishment of principal American labor unions, procedures that unions use to gain benefits for their members, the effects of unionization, the minimum wage, and unemployment insurance.

2. Describe the current economy and labor market, including the types of goods and services produced, the types of skills workers need, the effects of rapid technological change, and the impact of international competition.

3. Discuss wage differences among jobs and professions, using the laws of demand and supply and the concept of productivity.

4. Explain the effects of international mobility of capital and labor on the U.S. economy.

12.5 Students analyze the aggregate economic behavior of the U.S. economy.

1. Distinguish between nominal and real data.

2. Define, calculate, and explain the significance of an unemployment rate, the number of new jobs created monthly, an inflation or deflation rate, and a rate of economic growth.

3. Distinguish between short-term and long-term interest rates and explain their relative significance.

12.6 **Students analyze issues of international trade and explain how the U.S. economy affects, and is affected by, economic forces beyond the United States's borders.**

1. Identify the gains in consumption and production efficiency from trade, with emphasis on the main products and changing geographic patterns of twentieth-century trade among countries in the Western Hemisphere.

2. Compare the reasons for and the effects of trade restrictions during the Great Depression compared with present-day arguments among labor, business, and political leaders over the effects of free trade on the economic and social interests of various groups of Americans.

3. Understand the changing role of international political borders and territorial sovereignty in a global economy.

4. Explain foreign exchange, the manner in which exchange rates are determined, and the effects of the dollar's gaining (or losing) value relative to other currencies.

Publications Available from the Department of Education

This publication is one of over 600 that are available from the California Department of Education. Some of the more recent publications or those most widely used are the following:

Item no.	Title (Date of publication)	Price
0973	The American Indian: Yesterday, Today, and Tomorrow (1991)	$8.75
1372	Arts Work: A Call for Arts Education for All California Students (1997)	11.25
1436	California Department of Education Early Start Program Guide (1998)	10.00
1461	California Public School Directory, 1999	19.50
1438	California School Accounting Manual, 1998 Edition	28.50
1398	California Year-Round Education Directory, 1997-98 (1998)	10.00
1439	Check It Out! Assessing School Library Media Programs (1998)	9.25
1281	Connect, Compute, and Compete: The Report of the California Education Technology Task Force (1996)	5.75
1132	Course Models for the History–Social Science Framework: Grade Seven—World History and Geography: Medieval and Early Modern Times (1994)	15.25
1389	English Language Arts Content Standards for California Public Schools, Kindergarten Through Grade Twelve (1998)	9.25
1244	Every Child a Reader: The Report of the California Reading Task Force (1995)	5.25
0804	Foreign Language Framework for California Public Schools, Kindergarten Through Grade Twelve (1989)	7.25
1064	Health Framework for California Public Schools, Kindergarten Through Grade Twelve (1994)	10.00
1284	History–Social Science Framework for California Public Schools, 1997 Updated Edition (1997)	12.50
1245	Improving Mathematics Achievement for All California Students: The Report of the California Mathematics Task Force (1995)	5.25
1024	It's Elementary! Elementary Grades Task Force Report (1992)	9.00
1442	Joining Hands: Preparing Teachers to Make Meaningful Home-School Connections (1998)	13.25
1107	Literature for History–Social Science, K–8 (1993)	9.00
1133	Map Resource Packet (1994)	3.00
1216	Martin Luther King, Jr. 1929–1968 (1995)	7.50
1474	Mathematics Framework for California Public Schools, Kindergarten Through Grade Twelve (1999)	17.50
1065	Physical Education Framework for California Public Schools, Kindergarten Through Grade Twelve (1994)	7.75
1462	Reading/Language Arts Framework for California Public Schools, Kindergarten Through Grade Twelve (1999)	17.50
1276	Teaching Reading: A Balanced, Comprehensive Approach to Teaching Reading in Prekindergarten Through Grade Three (1996)	5.75
1261	Visual and Performing Arts Framework for California Public Schools, Kindergarten Through Grade Twelve (1996)	15.00
1392	Work-Based Learning Guide (1998)	12.50
1390	Work Permit Handbook (1998)	13.00
1381	Workforce Career Development Model (1998)	9.50

Orders should be directed to:

California Department of Education
CDE Press, Sales Office
P.O. Box 271
Sacramento, CA 95812-0271

Please include the item number and desired quantity for each title ordered. Shipping and handling charges are additional, and purchasers in California also add county sales tax.

Mail orders must be accompanied by a check, a purchase order, or a credit card number, including expiration date (VISA or MasterCard only). Purchase orders without checks are accepted from educational institutions, businesses, and governmental agencies. Telephone orders will be accepted toll-free (1-800-995-4099) for credit card purchases. *All sales are final.*

Prices are subject to change. Please call 1-800-995-4099 for current prices and shipping charges.